Praise for *Leading with Respect*

"Revealing and inspiring, candid and engaging . . . After reading this book, you'll have learned some useful lessons."
—Christie Hefner, former chairman and CEO of Playboy Enterprises (from the foreword)

"A must-read that delivers enormous opportunity for anyone who wants to be successful in today's business world."
—Robert L. Dilenschneider, founder and CEO of The Dilenschneider Group and author of *Character, Decisions*, and *Nailing It*

"Marcy Syms takes us on a life journey with her through an American Dream. The book is filled with practical advice that we can all use as we embark on our own journeys."
—Dr. Georgette Bennett, founder of the Tanenbaum Center for Interreligious Understanding and author of *Religicide* and *Thou Shalt Not Stand Idly By*

"Invaluable! The stories in this book take our breath away."
—Muriel Fox, co-founder of the National Organization for Women

"Marcy Syms shares the wisdom she learned through her personal leadership journey from founder's daughter to CEO to philanthropist. It's pure Marcy—authentic and from the heart. Don't miss this remarkable book."
—Carolyn Carter, Global President, International Women's Forum

"Respect isn't just a value—it's a strategy. In *Leading with Respect*, Marcy Syms shares how she built a retail empire by putting people first. Equal parts inspiring and practical, this

book will leave you thinking differently about leadership, business, and what it really takes to succeed."
—**Gary B. Cohen**, Managing Partner of CO2 Coaching; author of *Just Ask Leadership: Why Great Mangers Always Ask the Right Questions*

"Skip your MBA and just read these pages. It's inspiring, heartfelt, relatable and has gems on each page."
—**Jamie Keane**, founder of Be Spotted, Julip, and Dog Spotted Marketing

"Marcy Syms, who became the youngest female NYSE company president, shares candid lessons from four decades of leadership while staying true to the core promise of respect—for customers, employees, and brands."
—**Allen Adamson**, co-founder of Metaforce; author of *Seeing the How: Transforming What People Do, Not Buy, to Gain Market Advantage*

"Learning through story is so much more rich and long lasting than learning by being told what to do or how to do it. Marcy Syms is an excellent narrator, weaving stories from different parts of her life to demonstrate that respect is foundational to leadership."
—**Dr. Fredda Herz Brown,** founding partner of Relative Solutions; author of *The Essential Roadmap: Navigating Family Enterprise Sustainability in a Changing World*

"Marcy Syms provides treasured advice and wisdom as she shares her insights and valuable lessons learned in this book."
—**Richard Tereo**, Director, Corporate Administration and Spirit of Children Foundation, Spencer Spirit Holdings, Inc.

"A fresh and candid account of how capitalism works in America . . . *Leading with Respect* is more than a business school case study, it is the whole course!"
—**Sheila Riggs**, Member, Board of Directors, Benco Dental

"It's a rare business book that is both useful and endearing at the same time. Through her clear-eyed personal stories, Marcy illuminates how an entrepreneurial business evolved through changing times but always held to its core principles. Here is practical wisdom from a woman who really understands human nature."
—**Irene R. Miller**, former CFO and Vice-Chairman, Barnes & Noble, Inc.

"Marcy Syms takes you inside the heads of two groundbreaking businesspeople: herself, and her father Sy. Peppered with vivid stories and adept reflections."
—**Dr. Noam Wasserman**, Dean, Yeshiva University's Sy Syms School of Business

"Foundational principles of integrity, leadership, education, and most of all respect are not just theoretical for Marcy—they are the very bedrock upon which her career has been built. A must-read for anyone striving to build a leadership style that is both ethical and impactful."
—**J.J. Sussman**, International Director, The Gesher Organization

Also by Marcy Syms

Mind Your Own Business and Keep It in the Family

LEADING
WITH
RESPECT

Adventures of an
Off-Price Fashion Pioneer

Marcy Syms

President of the Sy Syms Foundation

Foreword by Christie Hefner

CITADEL PRESS
Kensington Publishing Corp.
kensingtonbooks.com

CITADEL PRESS BOOKS are published by

Kensington Publishing Corp.
900 Third Avenue
New York, NY 10022

All Kensington titles, imprints, and distributed lines are available at special quantity discounts for bulk purchases for sales promotions, premiums, fund-raising, educational, or institutional use. Special book excerpts or customized printings can also be created to fit specific needs. For details, write or phone the office of the Kensington sales manager: Kensington Publishing Corp., 900 Third Avenue, New York, NY 10022, attn: Sales Department; phone 1-800-221-2647.

Library of Congress Control Number: 2025935037

First hardcover printing: September 2025
ISBN: 978-0-8065-4481-6

ISBN: 978-0-8065-4442-7 (e-book)

10 9 8 7 6 5 4 3 2 1

Printed in the United States of America

The authorized representative in the EU for product safety and compliance is eucomply OU, Parnu mnt 139b-14, Apt 123
Tallinn, Berlin 11317, hello@eucompliancepartner.com

To L.R.L.

Contents

Christie Hefner, former chairman and CEO of Playboy Enterprises

Before the phrases *stakeholder capitalism* and *servant leadership* entered the business vernacular, Sy and Marcy Syms were building a company based on those values. This recounting of that journey—especially Marcy's four decades as a CEO, a philanthropist, and an activist is revealing and inspiring.

I first met Marcy more than three decades ago, through an organization of women business leaders called the Committee of 200 (C200). It brought together women entrepreneurs and corporate executives. We facilitated the exchange of ideas about how to succeed and change the environment so that more women could get ahead. From the first times we were together, it was clear to me that Marcy was a driven, no-nonsense, yet full-of-fun woman. She would have succeeded at whatever she set her mind to.

Marcy has written a candid and engaging book. On the business side, she shares the challenges of working with her father. She is honest about how it required seeking outside professional help to manage that relationship, and about their disagreement over merging with Filene's. On the personal side, she shares her own serious health challenges and her sense of failure when the company's public offering didn't turn out as expected.

When Marcy asked me to write this foreword, I was flattered by her trust in me. I wasn't sure, though, that I was the right person. So, I asked to read the book before agreeing. Once I did, I couldn't help but be struck by so many similarities. My father launched *Playboy* magazine in 1953, six years before Sy started Syms. In Marcy's portrait of her dad, I saw much that reminded me of my own father's. The scrupulous attention to detail. The certainty in their own point of view. The willingness to take risks from the beginning: Sy literally gambled and won a trifecta; Hef mortgaged our furniture twice to raise funds to start the magazine. Both of their appreciation for the idea of not just building a business, but building a brand. And their ability to create cultures that felt more like family than just coworkers. The vision to see and believe in what hadn't been done before. The overarching respect for the customer, or reader.

Moreover, Marcy's path and mine have had similarities. Growing up, neither of us intended to go into the family business. We both had other interests. Consequently, neither of us sought an MBA, though I'd argue that we both learned management by walking around (sometimes called an MBWA). We both supplemented our education and experience by taking additional courses like "Finance for the Non-Financial Executive," and joining the Young Presidents' Organization (YPO).

We both had extraordinarily long tenures as CEO, each during turbulent times: Marcy served for fifteen years; I served for twenty. We both focused on maintaining the legacy of the original brand's values, while professionalizing what had been an entrepreneurial founder–led company.

In each case, our fathers were stunningly casual about broaching the subject of our taking over. Her insights about how working with her father as founder required both creative compromise and effective communication felt very familiar to me.

On a lighter note, Marcy was named for a popular Arrow shirt collar, as Arrow was an important brand early on to Syms. Fittingly, Arrow was one of *Playboy* magazine's earliest fashion advertisers. One of the best birthday presents I ever bought my dad was a Sulka smoking jacket—a look that became a part of *Playboy* iconography. I learned from this book that Sulka was a company Syms owned for a number of years.

I especially identified with that feeling that is both exhilarating and scary as hell when you're put into a position that you aren't yet qualified for. Marcy writes of taking solace from the opening line from Dr. Spock's famous baby book, *You know more than you think you do*. I am fond of quoting a line often attributed to T.S. Eliot, *How do you know how tall you are, if you're not in over your head*. In both of our cases, we committed to continuing to learn as we went. That commitment to being a lifelong learner is one of Marcy's singular strengths.

But you don't need to have had similar life experiences to relate to this book. Her Rules of Customer Service are relevant to many businesses today. Everyone can benefit from reading about her techniques for interviewing candidates, as well as how to be attentive to what your boss responds to when you are seeking approval . . . or a raise. Moreover, I dare the reader not to laugh out loud when she reads "The Top Ten Things Only Women Understand."

There's much here to learn about negotiating deals and assessing mergers and acquisitions. Marcy is direct in sharing what she wishes the company had done differently. And in a time when there is much focus on innovation, Marcy's understanding that entrepreneurship is the ultimate team sport is spot-on.

After reading this book, I believe that you'll not only have learned some useful lessons, but will also feel that you've gotten to know the remarkable Marcy Syms.

PROLOGUE

Breathe. Let go. And remind yourself that this very moment
is the only one you have for sure.
—Oprah Winfrey

I wrote this book to share the lessons I've learned in more than four decades as a woman in business, as a CEO, as a philanthropist, and as an activist.

The thread running through all my experience is the critical importance of respect. From an early age, I was taught to respect others and expect respect in return. My father and I built a business based on respect for customers, clothing manufacturers, and our employees. Respect for their time, respect for their intelligence, respect for their hard-earned money, and respect for their diverse opinions.

This principle has guided me as I ran and then painfully reorganized an NYSE company, as I run a large charitable foundation, as I found myself being the principal caregiver for a sister, brother, and mother at the ends of their lives, and as I devote myself now to activism and education on behalf of women who start and run their own businesses.

My career has truly been eclectic.

Our slogan at Syms was: *An educated consumer is our best customer.* I hope the stories and information in this book make you a more educated reader and help you make the decisions that will shape your career and your life.

On one of my rare vacations not created from adding a few days on to the end of a business trip, I planned to be at the Aspen Institute. One of the founders of the institute, Mortimer Adler, was conducting a session for executives on the Great Books. The focus was going to be philosophy, a subject on which Adler was a recognized authority. At the time, the only thing I knew about philosophical writers of the past was Aristotle's discussion about a life well lived. Aspen was beautiful. The other members of the seminar session were exemplary members of the business community.

I was experiencing the transition of leaving a marriage and finding my footing as a single woman who also happened to be the COO and president of a public company. Somehow all the factors that brought me to that moment created the need for me to try something daring, new, and defining. I decided hang gliding was just the thing to scratch that itch.

After one lesson on the ground with an instructor, I was lifted to the side of a mountain and strapped in with headgear and clear directions on how to get from the mountain's edge to the airport in Hayden. As soon as I was airborne, instead of feeling exhilaration I only felt nausea. As the glider was embraced by the wind, I saw little I could do to control the outcome.

I had to go with it and somehow rise to the occasion without paralyzing panic. I feared I was going to throw up and once on the ground, was going to be an unspeakable mess. Somehow, I touched down at the airport, the glider stopped moving, and a person on each side helped me out of the seat. I asked for a bag and promptly gave up my breakfast.

I've often thought back on this experience in relation to challenging oneself and being able to work through panic. Working with a father I adored and respected and always wanted to make happy was exciting and challenging. I've had many challenges over the last forty years. Some, like the hang gliding, were situations I've brought on myself. Others

came about through the circumstances and environment sur-
rounding me. We have all experienced such times in our lives.
The very essence of who we are sees us through to the next
moment, when life isn't so threatening.

I hope you'll find inspiration, comfort, and renewed energy through my story.

INTRODUCTION

Don't let the bad guys win.
—Sy Syms

A small, typed copy of my father's quote has hung for a long time on the wall above my desk. It serves as a reminder of his determination to succeed. It's also been my motto for a long time. I don't regard it as aggressive; I regard it as demanding respect.

Syms, the retailer founded by my father, Sy Syms, in 1959—which I had the good fortune to run from 1998 until 2013—changed the way retailers treated their customers by emphasizing the notion of respect for their intelligence, time, and pocketbook. My dad's marketing slogan, used for forty years in our radio and TV and print ads, was *An Educated Consumer is our Best Customer.* We applied it to everything we did.

His big idea was simple: Become so important to your suppliers that they want to help you grow. He often said that if he went out of business, the consumer would forget Syms and find somewhere else to shop, but that the clothing industry had nowhere else to go because we were important to manufacturers' profitability.

He realized that in order for us to grow, the customer must have a unique experience. That meant offering the best bargains with the nicest and most knowledgeable sales-people, in a store that always respected their intelligence.

From these concepts we grew our brand. Armed with those lessons and our name, respect was the leitmotif in everything I've done in my life.

The name Syms became synonymous with getting a great deal on your clothes. Sy was proud his name had become used like that. "I wish everyone could be a noun someday," he once said.

This book will show you exactly how we made this happen. The lessons I learned from my father, from our employees, from our customers, from other family-owned businesses, and from women entrepreneurs changed my life. The experiences I'll relate range from the exhilarating to the difficult to the tragic. I hope you'll find them enlightening and inspiring—and I hope especially that the positive messages I try to bring to all of them might help you start or grow your own businesses or motivate you to start the nonprofit you've always thought about but never got around to. That's my goal.

The Syms brand lives on mainly through philanthropy now, but the Syms legacy can be seen in countless outlet malls and in the endless choice in price and quality offered by online retailers. Those options wouldn't have happened in the same way without the ideas brought to market by my father and which I carried on.

Syms, the store and the man, taught me lessons in both business and life. I hope my sharing them will help you find useful resonances with your own story. These lessons start with respect for employees, customers, and manufacturers, and range from scrupulous attention to detail—down to the exact location of every piece of merchandise over every counter in every store—strict honesty with employees, suppliers, and customers, including detailed price tags and fabric information, color-coded price tags that enabled customers to find their size easily on different products around the store, and the best prices anywhere for quality, name-brand goods.

The Syms story holds lessons that reverberate today. While Syms is no longer in the retail business, its model of giving consumers easy, informed access to products they want has been adapted by companies ranging from Amazon to Zappos. Syms was also a pioneer in outsourcing some production to China for a short time, with our so-called "SSS" or private-label, natural fiber products, occasionally with comic results.

The Syms story is really the story of how smart marketing led to higher living standards and prosperity. It's a snapshot of savvy and determined entrepreneurship succeeding in a fascinating time period—the early 1960s and 1970s—just as communications and technological breakthroughs shrunk the world.

It's above all a story of respect, especially for me. Earning the respect of my father as I rose in the business taught me to respect and try to understand all of my coworkers, as well as customers and suppliers, as people. You have to show that you're willing to work harder and smarter, appreciate those who try to keep up to your standards, and reward those who exceed them.

These lessons also prepared me for life post-Syms. My later work on boards, philanthropic organizations, and political issues arose from my respect for people—especially women—and their needs and aspirations, problems, and goals.

We'll look in detail at how my father, helped by me and others along the way, grew Syms from a couple of stores in Manhattan to create the first truly off-price clothing stores by meeting the needs of manufacturers and consumers at the same time. It's a story about a particularly interesting moment in retailing and contains lessons that we see reflected in business headlines to this day. We planted seeds that will bear fruit well into the future.

A key moment from my time at Syms stands out in my

mind as representative of the values at the heart of the whole enterprise. Some years ago, due to a last-minute paperwork error, we didn't have the right permits to open a new suburban New Jersey store on the appointed day. Rather than send home hundreds of disappointed people, who likely would never come back when we did open, my dad and I commandeered a car hood in the parking lot and wrote out $10 discount coupons for everybody.

We ordinarily never did sales except for a twice-yearly Bash. We wound up getting nearly all of the customers back when the store finally opened and made lots of new friends who felt pretty special after learning our off-price rule of *no coupons*. We learned an important lesson—that if we respected the customer by making good on our mistake, in turn they would respect us.

You'll meet my truly remarkable father through my stories, as well as from never-published interviews he gave for a never-published book in the 2000s. I'm biased, of course, but I think you'll agree that he deserves a lot of credit as a major twentieth-century retail innovator. In any event, you'll become an educated reader and can decide for yourself.

I hope you'll enjoy the details of how a Syms store was organized and operated. Sy's original idea was simple and brilliant: buy the overruns, seconds, and last-season fashions of the biggest brand names, like Gant, Jockey, and London Fog, helping them get rid of unwanted inventory after they had made their profit earlier in the season. Syms could buy all this merchandise at maybe 25 percent off the wholesale price, and sell it within 10 percent of the wholesale price, running the business at a 35 percent markup. A win-win!

You'll learn how we chose our locations (near big population centers, near interstate highways, and near at least one shopping center). You'll see how the careful design and placement of shelving and counters enabled us to display the merchandise consumers wanted in convenient places, and we'll decipher the color-coded tags each piece bore, including the seemingly inscrutable series of numbers they each carried. We'll read some of the Syms Training Manual, which lays out clearly what was expected of each "educator" and how each rule contributed to our respect for the customer's time and money, and made each "educator" greeting our customers more valuable to those customers and to themselves.

Over the years I've come to realize how much Syms meant to our customers. They ranged from commuters needing suits for the office to women, especially, who wanted to add authentic designer outfits for career dressing at reasonable prices. I was touched recently at an event at Harvard, where I participated as an Advanced Leadership Institute Fellow, when a woman I didn't know looked at my name tag and exclaimed: "Marcy Syms! I loved shopping at Marcy's Place!"

Marcy's Place was a discrete section in our bigger stores (that my father named) for higher-end goods needing more security, like a $2000 Gucci bag we offered for $499. We also operated A. Sulka & Co., the highest-end bespoke men's haberdashery on two continents, until we sold it to Richemont Holdings, which also owned Dunhill and Montblanc.

While we were riding high, we went public on the New York Stock Exchange at thirty times earnings. Our ticker symbol was SYM, of course. I became the youngest female president of an NYSE company. I'll share a number of lessons from this time and reflect on what it meant to be the only woman in the room for negotiations, meetings, and press conferences.

Eventually the manufacturers started making merchandise specifically tailored to their own retail outlets, which sprung up largely as a real estate play in the 1990s. They were called factory outlets. The outlets drew customers because they contained stores with labels like Coach, Ralph Lauren, Liz Claiborne, and Nike. Gradually, the supply of off-price merchandise we could get shrank and Syms suffered.

The lessons from our extended reorganization include the need to stay focused on the needs of stakeholders, treating everyone fairly, even when that proved difficult. Patience and calm are often overlooked virtues.

After the reorganization I had both the time and, thanks to the Sy Syms Foundation, the wherewithal to devote my time to nonprofits and political issues in which I felt could make a real difference to the lives of women. I was mentored by remarkable women and I've tried to return the favor to the next generation.

Syms was a company with a family culture, for all the good and the difficulty those words entail. We'll look at some lessons that apply to all family businesses. I believe the joys of running a family business outweigh the almost inevitable sorrows, but we'll look at both.

I'll offer lessons from my post-Syms life serving on boards of directors, in order to explain how even one director can exert huge influence, whether on a family business or on General Motors. Board membership gives an individual both great insight and great power to create change. Decisions by directors, and their influence on other directors, can establish a new food pantry where it's needed in an underserved neighborhood, fire the CEO, and anything in between. I'll discuss the health-related philanthropy Syms has championed since Sy developed heart disease many years ago, and my particular interest in encouraging research into the very different symptoms women show in heart disease and other maladies. There's been some progress, but much more needs to be done.

I'll also offer practical advice on how women can build a wardrobe that commands respect in the workplace without breaking the bank. I'll spend some time on another issue close to my heart: How women can become thriving entrepreneurs despite the still formidable obstacles thrown in our paths. I'll also share insights into caregiving, which has occupied a lot of my energy in recent years, as it often does for women in the workplace.

Finally, I'll talk about recharging our mental and physical batteries, as I was fortunate enough to be able to do at Harvard recently, and prepare ourselves for the next chapter in our lives.

CHAPTER 1

Educating Me

Happiness is not a goal, it is a by-product.
—Eleanor Roosevelt

The vivid memories of my childhood that I retain reflect the environment that made me the person I am. One of my first memories was playing, sometimes alone and sometimes with the neighbor kid, Larry, in the elevator in our building at 1616 Newkirk Avenue in Brooklyn. My recently born brother Stephen was taking up most of Mom's time, so I was left to my own devices during the day.

I loved pushing elevator buttons. I—or we, if Larry was around—went up and down, not disturbing anybody. I liked being the one to push the buttons, though I could only reach up to 4, while Larry could go all the way to 10. Each of the bare, black-and-white tiled floor landings had different smells, depending on what was cooking.

Whenever an adult got on, we pretended to be the elevator operators and asked for their floor, and I would push the button. This always elicited smiles and pleasant chatter. It sounds trivial, but this pleased people. It was a small service. The smiles just reinforced our pleasure. It was a pleasant playtime game. I loved doing it and never forgot it. This is probably my first memory.

When I was an infant, we shared an apartment with my mother's parents. We all three slept in the living room of a fourth-floor walk-up in the Bronx. It was across the street from a great regional park that my mother's father, Louis Glickman, had worked on as part of the Depression-era Works Progress Administration. That's where I learned to ride a bike, play shuffleboard with old retired men, and just hang out. I remember tough-looking guys hanging around smoking and talking about the union or baseball or politics. The neighborhood was pretty rough. You needed a good reason to go out, especially with those four flights of stairs waiting for you.

My mother's parents had very little, but as people did in those days, they bought as much stock as they could in AT&T, the "widows and orphans" stock, which was safe and paid a nice dividend. They sold it in 1959 to invest in Sy's first store. They adored Sy and had great faith in him.

Even though I was very little, I still remember the faith they had in him and how much that meant to the family. Loyalty is in some sense a part of respect.

My grandmother was the first woman I saw and heard express her pride in getting a job, which was in a shoe store. She became the assistant manager. She often told me, when we were alone, that I needed to make my own living. Be independent. This was way before feminism and before I knew anything about Susan B. Anthony or the suffragettes. I got this message from my bubbe, a Romanian immigrant. It stuck early.

Our first real house was on Lee Avenue in Yonkers, about thirty minutes north of New York City. My first glimpse of it came as I was perched on my dad's shoulders while we walked up the pathway. To the young me it looked like a fairy house from the Jack and Jill books that I devoured. It had a yard! It had an upstairs! I thought this was heaven.

In the 1950s this section of Yonkers was for up-and-coming commuters. Our block had Germans, Jamaicans, Italians, Irish, French, you name it. It was like the UN and it was fabulous. It seemed everybody, like Sy, had used the GI Bill to buy their first home. They were all young parents, which was great for me because of all the kids. These were first-generation Americans and very entrepreneurial. Having made it through World War II, often by working, the women, now homemakers and mothers, knew they had an important part to play in the economy and the culture.

Our neighborhood was a great place and a wonderful time to be a kid. I was raised to respect my elders, not blindly, but because of their accomplishments, because they knew more than I did and I could learn from them. My friends all seemed to feel the same way. I didn't know it then, but I realize now that respect and aspiration were woven into my behavior as I was growing up.

My kindergarten teacher, Miss Nutmeg (really!), was of mixed race. She was beautiful; I thought she looked like a princess. Kindergarten taught me my first lesson in the difference between boys and girls. Every morning we'd all lie on our little mats and take a nap. All the girls, that is. The boys couldn't stop moving. Some never napped. Miss Nutmeg let this all play out without losing her cool, as long as they didn't bother us. This taught me early on that rules should accommodate what people are able to do. It didn't make sense to yell at the boys to go to sleep when they simply couldn't.

I thrived on story time and loved learning new things. Later, my interest in English literature and reading introduced me to people and situations I hadn't experienced. I always found it exciting to live these situations in my imagination.

As school continued and Mom had children every two years, my responsibilities at home grew. By the time Dad went into business for himself, I was very occupied by chores. I found all the vacuuming, dishwashing, laundry, and especially washing the cloth diapers tedious. With all my young siblings it seemed to never stop. I wanted to be helpful to my mother, especially after she suffered postpartum depression after her third child.

At age five I used what maternal instincts I had to care for my brother Robert. It was a joy to be able to give him my love. I think my experiences at that age were decisive in my becoming a feminist, even before I knew that word.

Before my mom gave birth to her sixth child, she needed to get the approval of three doctors, plus her husband and to see a psychiatrist, to have her tubes tied after the birth. I was eleven. I remember the stress and sadness, trying to understand. I knew how babies were made and the process made me feel humiliated for my mother. She had little power over her destiny. All the psychiatrists and doctors were men. How could they understand? Back then, there were very few women doctors.

I knew from that point that it was crucial for society to have more women doctors. The feeling you're not wanted is a terrible burden. One that gratefully none of us knew.

I was always an organizer. Maybe because I was the oldest child, or maybe just enjoying responsibility that others looked to me for, I was often asked, "What are we gonna do next?" In fifth grade a few of us girls started the bumblebees club. We shared experiences, started to notice boys, and did a few good works. We set up a lemonade stand. It was fun to bring refreshments to help the kids playing baseball in the park to cool off, and the boys noticed our kindness.

One of the girls in our class wanted to be in our little

group, but the others didn't really like her. One day her mother came to speak to me, saying it was very important to her daughter to join our group. I was stunned that she had put me in this position, but I did get the girl into our group. It eventually broke up under the pressures of middle school.

I could have ignored the mother and not dealt with it. After all, I would need to sell the idea to the other girls. In choosing to take on the task, I learned that others, including adults, saw me as a person with empathy and compassion who could communicate in a way that would influence others. That's leadership.

Sy once presented me with a leadership award from New Jersey's Monmouth University at a banquet. He told the story of how when I was little, he would give me money to take my younger siblings to the movies. He always gave me enough for the tickets, popcorn, and treats, with a little left over. He said, "Not only did she come home on time with the younger kids, who got more candy, but—and this is what impressed me the most—she always brought home change."

At age twelve, the feminist in me was preoccupied with convincing my elders that I should get a bat mitzvah at our Conservative synagogue. This was not the practice in the early 1960s, at least not at Lincoln Park Jewish Center in Yonkers. Maybe because they all got tired of me asking, they finally gave me a Friday night service (rather than the usual Saturday service that the boys got). The women of the synagogue gave me a Bible with my name on the front, signed by the rabbi. I was encouraged, a few years later, when the bat mitzvah became routine in Reform and then Conservative temples.

Somewhat counterintuitively, I decided to run for office in middle school. My friend Lynn ran for treasurer. I didn't feel popular enough to run for an important position, so I ran for secretary. Janet Rose, the prettiest girl in our grade, ran against me. I don't know if she was smarter than me, but she was prettier, and I figured all the boys would vote for her. So, Lynn and I created banners, flyers, a whole campaign. We actually won. Although we never really did anything while in office, the campaign added to my self-esteem. My biggest takeaway was that it doesn't really matter how pretty you are, you'd better have something to say. Janet might've got them on first impression, but my job was to get them on the second look. It was a good lesson.

I also learned from not having to do anything as secretary that it was nonetheless important to have a platform. Kids would ask my opinion on things because I won the election. I really enjoyed opining on lunchroom food choices, or whether the library should allow taking out a fifth book. This was my first platform.

The Syms family was now six kids and two adults stuffed in a one-bathroom house, significantly near Yonkers Raceway, where the trotters trotted. With his own store open, Sy had been saving money for a down payment on a house in Bronxville. Sy loved to "do the math" with the trotter books that included stats on horse and jockey performance. He would scribble down numbers and choose which horse he would bet on. Betting was part of his personality. He was fortunate that unlike most bettors, he ended up in the plus column year after year.

We moved to a ten-room house thanks to a trifecta that he won, picking the first, second and third horses in one race, in order. He won $27,000 (about $270,000 today). Even after having to give some to the two huge thugs waiting for him outside the ticket window, he had enough for a down payment on a five-bedroom, five-bath house in Bronxville. It was a beautiful Georgian colonial formerly owned by a president of Reynolds aluminum who got transferred.

Seeing it for the first time, I thought I was starring in a Disney Sunday night show with Tinker Bell and Snow White. But the move turned out to be the worst decision they ever made. My siblings and I were the only Jews in the school district, and even though we were only eighteen miles from Grand Central, it felt like another planet. We later found out that a petition to keep us out of the school system got a lot of support, but failed to be implemented.

My parents at first were sure everyone would just get along and work out their differences, as had been our experience in Yonkers. In Bronxville we experienced physical threats and life-changing anti-Semitism. The prejudices we encountered ultimately made me prouder of my Jewishness and bolder about showing it in public. Being Jewish was not something that would make me cower or apologize or not want to be what I was, and I always tried to be genuine. I started wearing a small gold Star of David on a very delicate chain around my neck. Eventually, everyone in my classes knew what it meant.

During high school I purposely did things that didn't come naturally to me. I went out for cheerleading despite neither being athletic nor having a cheerleader's body. I learned and practiced cheerleading moves for months before the tryout and spent every night in a hot bath with Epsom salts to sooth the resulting pain. I was damned if I was going to show my classmates that I couldn't do this. I made the team and some of my friends let me avoid doing the tumblesaults, which I couldn't master. My smaller repertoire of moves made my position more of a mascot than a full team member, but I was delighted as the most vertically challenged cheerleader to always start the cheers.

I made some good friends, but it was very difficult being confronted with irrational prejudice and deep-rooted assumptions about what I could or couldn't do or how I was supposed to behave. The prevailing stereotypes were everywhere I turned. I've never forgotten this and have always tried to be open-minded when dealing with colleagues and friends. First impressions matter, but assumptions can lead you astray.

I had many conversations with Sy about the bullying and prejudice. I told him it was getting hard to get up and go to school. My two brothers would be provoked into fights and we were all called hurtful names. I couldn't relax. His advice: For the rest of the semester, treat high school like a job. If things don't get better by May, we'll move.

Once two boys stood outside Miss Babcock's biology class and through the glass door shouted some nonsense about seeing me making out in a car in the parking lot. I had never even kissed a guy at that point, much less in a parked car in the school parking lot. Everyone heard this, but nobody did anything. Miss Babcock paused a second or two and went right on talking about the digestive system. I remember because of my nausea from a fear response.

I found out that authorities might talk a good game about protecting you, but you ultimately have to protect yourself.

Senior year I was president of the choral group and assistant advertising manager of the school paper. I also starred in school plays and musicals. I was on the cheerleading squad, but couldn't perform much due to illness. I was probably overcompensating for wanting to scream, "You're wrong about us. You are ignorant."

The summer before senior year I went to Europe by myself. One of Sy's original tailors had family in Lugano, Switzerland, and I persuaded my parents to let me go visit them. The trip was an amazing experience for me. My hosts were an elderly couple who had me sleep on a cot in their crowded workroom, next to the sewing machines, steamers, and cutting tables. It was fantastic. I was exposed to new sights and tastes and flavors. I went to Florence to see relatives of our neighbors, taking a train to their summer place on the Mediterranean. Three weeks in Europe on my own opened my eyes to many things I never sensed or felt or thought were possible.

Once I got back to school the stress was just too much. My body broke down. At age sixteen I was diagnosed with a rare autoimmune disease known as pemphigus vulgaris. I had painful blisters throughout my mucus membranes and eventually on my skin. For a time, I was on a liquid diet. A neighbor and family friend, an ear, nose, and throat specialist named Lee Arnold, thought my symptoms looked like something he saw years earlier in a medical book. He contacted the retired head of New York Hospital's dermatology department, Dr. Arthur Grace, who studied rare diseases, and asked if I could see him. After a biopsy he put me in the hospital right away, but not before telling me the name of the disease and the likelihood it may be fatal.

I was in the hospital for nearly three months, treated with huge doses of the steroid cortisone, and endured a bunch of side effects. But I got a little better and was able to finish high school through a remote telephone hookup. While in the hospital I was very isolated. Because the steroids completely devastated my immune system, I could have no visitors except my parents and Dr. Grace.

During the time I was there, Dr. Grace's wife of fifty-five years was dying of cancer two floors above my room. He visited me every day after spending time with her, and our conversations were inspiring for me. He brought me great literature to read and then he would discuss it with me. He told me about the scientific conferences he had attended and all the travel he did for his work. He was the first person to make me feel intelligent in a way that would be important when navigating the outside world.

After leaving the hospital, I decided to not apply to Boston University as I had hoped. Instead, mostly due to my moon-face side effects from the steroids, I applied to women's colleges.

I decided on Chatham College in Pittsburgh. It is an excellent but relatively small liberal arts college with a beautiful campus—and most importantly, Dr. Grace said there was a doctor at the University of Pittsburgh Medical Center who was familiar with pemphigus and could supervise my medication regimen. Unfortunately, my symptoms became threatening by Thanksgiving, when I experienced a major outbreak. The doctor seemed to want to experiment with megadoses of vitamins to treat it. Well, I had already been down this path during the almost eighteen months I was trying to find a diagnosis, so I knew I was in jeopardy.

Back in New York, I met with Dr. Grace. I told him I wanted to get off cortisone. It turned out he had recently been to a conference in São Paolo, Brazil, on skin diseases. He had come back with information on methotrexate, a new wonder drug being experimentally used in chemotherapy for cancers. Eager to try something new, I was grateful to be introduced to a doctor who was willing to administer the drug for an off-label purpose. It worked and my sense of normalcy gradually returned. I was a guinea pig, but also the recipient of a miracle gift.

Despite a bad reaction that threw me back into the hospital, the disease seemed to go into remission. I've lived with it for fifty years.

I moved back home and applied to NYU and Finch College. It was unusual for a freshman to start in the spring semester of the first year, but both NYU and Finch accepted me after interviews. NYU did not offer me housing, so if I went there in Manhattan, I would need to commute to our family home. Finch was offering me housing, a roommate from Colorado, and a very welcoming admissions professional. Finch won hands down.

Let's pause my origin story for a bit to delve into the origin story of the company for which I worked for nearly thirty-five years—Syms. Its roots are my roots and it's a fascinating story.

CHAPTER 2

Educating Sy Syms

*Resiliency—not perfection, resiliency—that is the signature
of greatness.*
—Jim Collins

My father, born Seymour Merinsky in Brooklyn in 1926, was the youngest of eight children. Their Jewish parents had fled pogroms in Russia to emigrate to New York in 1904. They spoke mainly Russian and Yiddish.

My mother's father, Louis Glickman, came to the United States at five years old in steerage from Romania. He became a sheet metal worker and union organizer who was proud to be part of the construction of the Chrysler Building. Later in life, his favorite expression was that "all this will change when my ship comes in." He believed in fate. The formation of the labor unions was so important to my granddad's happiness that his expectations of how he fit into the master plan ultimately killed him. Unrealized dreams left him disillusioned, and he died a rather unfulfilled man. "Be careful of your expectations" was the lesson he passed on to me.

At the age of fifteen, Moishe, later Morris Merinsky, who had been conscripted into the Russian army at age thirteen, escaped in order take a boat to the New World. He landed at Ellis Island, the main immigration center in New York harbor, and moved in with a cousin who was living at 62 Delancey Street. The cousin, like many Jewish immigrants at the time, worked in the clothing business, often known as the rag trade, making a living by selling collars and cuffs.

Morris was a one-person American dream story. As soon as he arrived in America, he began earning money to bring his mother, two sisters, and a brother over as well.

Morris and his cousin decided to borrow some money and open a store in 1914 on Greenwich Street in lower Manhattan. After two years they had three stores—one on the Bowery, one on Orchard Street, and the one on Greenwich Street, offering men's furnishings in addition to the collars and cuffs.

After less than two years they had to file for bankruptcy. This wouldn't be Morris's first failure. If nothing else, Morris had determination and resilience. Between 1914 and 1927 he opened multiple stores with multiple partners and went through three separate bankruptcies, the last of which in 1927 was filed by Sophie Merinsky, my grandmother (whom I never met).

Following the assorted bankruptcies, Morris, who later shortened the family name to Merns, went into business as a distributor for Arrow shirts and Arrow collars, a leading men's clothing brand. After losing the Arrow business he eventually opened a men's clothing store in lower Manhattan with his son George, who was sixteen years Sy's senior.

While I was able to piece together family history from public records and newspaper files, my father never knew these details. All he ever said about my grandfather was that he sold collars and cuffs with Sy's brother. Sy said his father was quiet, hardworking, and kind. "And sadly, he was never really engaged with his kids."

*   *   *

Sy said in a recorded interview in 2006, "I believe that I was born with certain genes. At one time my father was a very successful merchant. He was a distributor for Arrow collars and Arrow shirts, which was the biggest in the country then. I was born in a town house in Park Slope, Brooklyn, 980 Park Place. It was a lovely town house. We had a cook. We had a car and a chauffeur. I think we had a housekeeper."

A couple of years after Sy was born, his father lost his Arrow distributorship. In 1931 he had to start over as a store owner on Washington Street in lower Manhattan, at first selling men's collars supplied to him by kindly distributors he had worked with at Arrow. (Men's shirt collars used to be a big deal. Before the era of a Maytag in every home, men would simply put a fresh, detachable collar on their shirts each morning and didn't have to wash the whole shirt so often. Like the buggy whip, detachable collars were a product for a bygone era.) My father recalls working in this store when he was little.

My father always said he named me Marcy after one of the most popular Arrow collarstyles of his youth, worn by Herbert Hoover among others, and also after Morris.

His father died when Sy was eighteen, and his mother passed away the same year.

When my grandfather died, the store went to the eldest son, George, and Sy did not work for George full-time until he first pursued a career as a play-by-play sports announcer. But the store did provide part-time work for Sy for a few years while he pursued his dream.

Though his mother adored him and Sy was cherished, he found more in common with his six older sisters. They were his living encyclopedia on how to be what he dearly wanted to be: a young American. He looked to them for advice on how he should talk, where he should go, how he should dress.

To Sy, being an American was everything. I firmly believe Sy's relationships with his sisters made him comfortable with me as his business confidante and later successor.

Sy wasn't a big guy, but he was muscular and agile and co-ordinated. He loved sports. In high school he was a catcher, never a great student but always great at sports. He harbored thoughts of becoming a professional baseball player and join-ing a minor league team, but that idea didn't work out.

During high school, with the war in Europe raging, he joined the Army. He used to say that he was such a poor stu-dent in high school that he signed up because the Army would give you a high school diploma equivalent when you turned eighteen. He was stationed at Washington and Lee University in Virginia, which had been commandeered by the Army as a training facility. Because he was good at num-bers and spatial relationships, he entered the engineering training corps. During one of his training operations, work-ing on bridge repairs, he had an accident and was diagnosed with a concussion. As this was near the end of the war, he was never deployed.

As soon as he could, he left the military and used the GI Bill to enroll in New York University. NYU had, and still has, an outstanding communications department. Sy took advan-tage of the school's then state-of-the-art radio studios (and nascent TV studios) to pursue his love of sports and to try to become a sports announcer. Sports were his passion and he listened to any game he could find on the radio. He would also practice for six hours a day, using a reel-to-reel tape recorder, the flat accent common among announcers of the day, in an attempt to lose his pronounced Brooklyn accent and enunciate like a Midwesterner. He largely succeeded, though once in a while a little Flatbush would slip through.

In both high school and college he didn't really like academics—he used to tell me he was a solid C—but he was facile with both numbers and spatial relationships, as even the Army had realized. Those skills would later help him quickly calculate the value of deals and design our stores.

He also had a vast amount of what we now call emotional intelligence. Seemingly without effort, he was able to establish relationships of respect and trust with employees, clients, and suppliers. His intelligence just wasn't traditional school stuff.

Sy also learned how to negotiate on the streets of Brooklyn, got into fights, was called a kike and a Jewboy. He learned how to hold his own. He used to tell me that outwitting someone is better than fighting, but you can't let them know you're afraid of a fight.

While at NYU he landed a radio job in New York reading the Associated Press news ticker at the half-hour breaks between midnight and 6 a.m. The opportunity came to him because my mother, Ruth, was a singer on this station and got him an interview. Ruth Glickman was another American dream story: the child of Romanian immigrants, she grew up in the Bronx in a five-story walk-up. At age sixteen she was working for two radio stations, WINS and WMCA, as the singer for their live orchestras.

Sy left New York for an offer of a play-by-play and general sports reporter job at radio station WLYK in Cumberland, a city nestled between Frostburg and Flintstone in northwestern Maryland. He did so well there that management offered him a four-hour show six days a week, mainly covering sports but incorporating other news. In full-page newspaper ads they billed it as *The Greatest Sports Show in Radio History!*

He left Cumberland for the bigger market of Charleston, West Virginia, but he got laid off in early 1950 when a coal miners' strike shut down the area's main industry. Looking for another job, in March 1950 he went to some open mic auditions in New York City. While waiting to be called to the microphone, he saw men twice his age who all seemed better at announcing than he was. Then and there he gave it up. He didn't want to spend time on something that wasn't going to add up to anything. "I'm outta here," he told my mother. He later described this as a major turning point in his life.

That's when he decided to join George at the family store in lower Manhattan. It was a discount store, like countless such storefront businesses strewn across New York and other big cities and small towns. Many were run by European immigrants seeking to make their way in the new country.

Lower Manhattan was a bustling, vibrating hodgepodge of small electronic stores, auction houses, tiny restaurants, plumbing suppliers, commercial printers, corrugated box makers, and political party headquarters, all living cheek by jowl with Wall Street and the Hudson tubes joining Manhattan to New Jersey, as well as the Staten Island ferry, which went past Ellis Island.

In this mix were those who owned or rented small shops or worked in auction houses that sold auto parts and construction material. It was a then–modern-day Middle Eastern bazaar with a vibrancy—constant chatter in the streets—fueled almost entirely by immigrants. I used to go as a little girl with my dad to a coffee shop on a Saturday morning. I still remember the cacophony of sounds and voices and accents and the smell of spicy fried food. If there were women around, I didn't see them—they were in the back office keeping the books.

Department stores would pay wholesale prices to manufacturers or their agents for goods, and then double the price for their retail customers. Wholesale prices then included the manufacturers' cost and profits. The Merns store, with its tiny twelve-foot frontage, was a classic discounter, paying wholesale for the same stuff, but marking it up maybe 25 percent instead of 50 percent, and thus accepting a lower profit margin on each sale. They could do this because they had cheaper rent and labor costs than the big stores.

Sy started as a salesman in his brother's store, but quickly took on all sorts of other responsibilities that proved to be great training for his future career. His personality made him a natural to become the store's buyer. In those days this was a key position. A good buyer develops close relationships with the suppliers, who can and often do offer a better quality or supply of garments to those they respect and trust and like. (Today, most orders are automated, taking the human element out of the equation. It's really different, and less dependent on personality.)

Sy was always respectful and customers loved him. His honesty led him to tell them all that he knew. He was a teacher and a leader. Each customer, in his eyes, was a messenger for what he was doing, so he had to explain it all to them. That's why they came back repeatedly and made sure he served them. They told their friends, who asked for Sy by name. He had an air of generosity and would frequently buy lunch for his staff on the spur of the moment.

As good as he was with customers, he was shy and never really hung out with the guys or went out for beers after work. While he rarely cultivated friendships, he was good at being available for friendly advice, especially with the vendors.

When the owner of Bill's Bar next door wanted to retire, Sy led the effort to expand the store to a then-respectable thirty-foot storefront. The store's success enabled the Merns boys to remodel the whole thing. The business also had two of Sy's sisters as important workers.

Eventually he got antsy working for George, who was sixteen years his senior, a Hollywood-handsome guy with a glamorous wife and lifestyle who didn't share Sy's vision, ambition, or work ethic. While George was at the barber or the local movie house, Sy would order the socks and underwear and keep both buyers and sellers happy.

By the late 1950s Sy thought he had a deal with this brother to buy 20 percent of the operation for $6,000, but this fell

apart. He set his sights on an elderly cousin's shop on Cort-
landt Street, which would require a $35,000 investment. He
didn't have it, but he found a partner in an older man, Irving
Pomerantz. Their 1,200-square-foot store opened on Hal-
loween in 1959.

Sy wanted to call the store Sy Merns, but his brother sued
him and won, so instead he contracted the names and called
it Sy Syms. He legally changed his name shortly thereafter.
Once Sy and George parted, they didn't speak again for
twelve years.

The new store bore a sign saying *Sy Syms* in the middle
and *Sy Merns* and *Irving Pomerantz* in smaller lettering below.
Nine years later Sy bought out Irving, who moved to an un-
related midtown store.

The $35,000 they paid for the store included roughly that
amount in inventory, mainly items manufacturers wanted to
unload. Sy would make his living selling garments manufacturers didn't want for the rest of his life.

Sy would often recount that he knew he was taking a
chance to go out on his own. The day he signed the contract
for the store, he said, he read a Sylvia Porter column in the
New York Post that said 83 percent of all new small businesses
fail. It turns out he was in the 17 percent.

The relatively nondescript storefront and floor-to-ceiling
racks of clothing foreshadowed the look of every Syms store
as we expanded over the years.

The store was next to the entrance to the Hudson Street
tubes that took thousands of New Jersey residents back and
forth to their Wall Street jobs each weekday. What could be
more convenient than to buy a shirt or pair of socks during
your lunch hour or on the way home? Sy liked to be on the
sales floor from noon to 2 p.m. to catch the lunch crowd.

He stocked the store with overruns and seconds and irregulars from big-name manufacturers, whom he convinced to
do business with him under the new model of "off-price."

While this practice later became common, he was the first to see the value in taking unwanted goods from big-name makers and selling them cheaply. From the start, he agreed not to mention the name brands in any advertising or outside signage. Customers wouldn't see brand names until they walked into the store. It was like a shared secret that they were getting a bargain. And it was a sign of respect for the manufacturers that he was valuing, rather than competing with, their brands. He was successful from the first day. Word of mouth kept a steady stream of new customers coming in.

As he later explained, "I'm only as good as the (brand) name I'm selling. So the name is of the utmost importance." The biggest name at first was Gant, the shirtmaker. "They were a very prestigious product. They were $8.50 at a store like Paul Stuart, and $2.99 at Syms. They were irregulars. Or we called them irregulars, but we gave a guarantee. If you find something that you don't like, we'll take it back from you. Without that guarantee, I'm not sure. But we had to tell them they were irregulars. That's where the educated consumer comes from. Tell them everything about the product you're selling them." He also often said that the most important thing was to "give customers a reason" to come to your shop. In Syms's case that reason was a combination of selection and price.

His old suppliers stuck with him and worked out deals for merchandise that was irregular or had a slight defect, returned items that department stores couldn't sell because the packaging had been damaged, the garments were last season's fashions, or they just didn't sell. All the merchandise came from brand-name designers.

From the beginning, Sy was completely honest about what he was selling.

In one of the interviews recorded in 2006, he said, "I always told the customer everything I knew, and it seemed to help. We got a lot of repeat business. When a man wanted a shirt or a tie, he knew where to go first. I consider honesty and communication very important. If you're in a bargain store, the more the customer knows, the more he's going to buy. If he had some background, knowing a Calvin Klein shirt normally goes for $75 or $100, he knows what he's getting." This was an early incarnation of the educated consumer.

Sy always believed that educating the consumer was the best way to keep on the good side of his suppliers. Their goods were being respected and new fans were being created. Sy knew that keeping suppliers happy meant keeping the goods flowing into his stores.

In those days, my dad recalled, the typical store owner stood behind the cash register all day and took cash and did pretty much nothing else. He also hired as many siblings, in-laws, nieces, and nephews as wanted a job. While this was generally considered a way to install trusted people in spots where they wouldn't steal from you, Sy did it because it created energy and enthusiasm. The manager, the most important person in the store, shouldn't be stuck behind the register all day. The cashier could do that. He wanted to be talking to as many people each day as he could. His relatives would also talk to people about him more than a nonfamily employee.

The off-price concept was a huge hit and Syms flourished. Between 1959 and 1969 he opened four more stores in Manhattan. His first slogan, *Unbelievable Syms*, eventually gave way to the *Educated Consumer is our Best Customer*, made famous by radio and TV ads starting in 1974.

The original slogan was both telling and important. Sy realized that price was the key. He could sell top-quality goods at prices well below what other retailers were charging, because of his relationships to and negotiations with the manufacturers. He was actually helping them by paying cash for inventory that was on their shelves at year-end, an influx that went straight to their bottom line, as well as clearing out unwanted inventory. As the years went by, Sy became convinced that the most important thing he was doing was keeping US clothing manufacturers in business by giving them cash for excess goods that would otherwise hurt their profits. He liked to say that if he went out of business, customers could easily find another clothing shop, but manufacturers couldn't find another buyer like him.

> "It's all in the buy," Sy used to say. At first he didn't understand how to explain this to his market. Hence the *Unbelievable Syms* slogan, referring to unbelievable prices. As he figured it out, he made the explaining, or educating, the central message. *An educated consumer is our best customer.*

Syms wasn't the first off-price store—Loehmann's had opened a store in Brooklyn in 1920—nor was it the last, with many imitators entering the fray in later years. But it was arguably the most dynamic and the concept that changed retailing the most.

Nearly a decade after he opened his store, Sy famously fought and lost, but really won, a battle with the mighty U. S. Steel Corporation. U.S. Steel wanted to buy out the store's lease and demolish it to build what is now One Liberty Plaza. In September 1969 *The Wall Street Journal* wrote a front-page article on Sy's David vs. Goliath battle, headlined SMALL HABERDASHERY UPSETS U.S. STEEL'S SKYSCRAPER PROJECT. SYMS' OWNER WANTS $100,000 TO BREAK NEW YORK LEASE: MEANWHILE, BUSINESS BOOMS. He didn't get his $100,000; the settlement was more like $24,000. But the publicity generated by a front-page story in the newspaper bible of his Wall Street clientele was, as another famous marketing phrase goes, priceless. He kept a framed copy of the story on his office wall.

Soon thereafter, two of his other stores in the neighborhood were ordered demolished under the eminent domain program that eventually created the site for the original World Trade Center campus. Sy moved into more spacious quarters at 45 Park Place.

From the beginning, the store specialized in underwear, socks, and other furnishings Sy could take off the manufacturers' hands at the end of each season. Their racks always included some sport coats and pants, but the trick was how to achieve a consistent flow of more kinds of apparel. The only way to have consistency of availability of a wide range of colors and sizes was to make deals at the beginning of the seasons, so Sy would commit to taking whatever fabric exclusives they had left and purchasing goods made with the leftover, already-paid-for fabric.

Sy would often need to commit to a certain volume — 20,000 pieces, say—in exchange for an exclusive on the white Worcester pinstripes, for example. He'd say he'd take all the fabric and the manufacturer would turn it into suits for Syms. He became more a part of the manufacturers' operations by committing to fabrics and delivery dates that worked for the brand. As an added incentive, he could assure them they'd never see any returns, because he knew he could find a price at which it would be an attractive buy.

"If we agree upon a price, you don't need to worry about returns. I'll sell them all," he would say. And he did. Manufacturers hated end-of-season returns because they ate directly into their profit. But Sy turned all this into cash for them. He was a popular guy. When he said, "I want to open more stores, will you work with me?" they said yes. He now needed to have lots of styles in all sizes. He became increasingly important to the biggest name brands.

After they moved into the Park Place store, Sy and his partner Irving Pomerantz expanded into a presentation of men's outerwear on the first three floors. They spent a lot of money on renovations, including an escalator and adding bathrooms and other amenities. Four dangerous steps to the first floor needed to be made safe. It was a construction site at the same time it was a working store.

The Park Place building was built in the 1880s. It had exposed pipes and creaky stairs that had to be rebuilt and made safe for public retail traffic. It housed small manufacturers and some offices, complete with some old-fashioned rolltop desks— one of which Sy took home.

The necessary renovations led to Sy's one and only deficit year—in 1974, when they put in an escalator and redid the basement.

Ever the marketer, Sy offered "escalator dividends" to compensate his customers for the inconvenience of renovations. In-store announcements enticed shoppers with lower prices for certain items for a limited time. These special offers weren't on the sales ticket and they changed every day, so you had to be there to see what the dividends would be. Years later, Kmart did the same thing with its Blue Light Specials. Sy didn't have any flashing lights.

The creation of the basement men's store required, among other things, building a big stairway in the middle of the store, demolishing parts of floors and ceilings where necessary. Eventually, the basement men's store enabled Sy and his educators to deal one-on-one with customers in a relatively quiet environment. Their personalized interaction led to more completed sales. More educators were stationed down there than anywhere else in the store. Within the black walls and sitting on the red carpeting were twenty-foot-long racks of suits ranging from 36 short to 48 extra-long, on each of three walls.

The impact when a customer saw this enormous selection of suits was overpowering, encouraging them to think, "My suit must be in there somewhere." Sy used to say, "If you can't find it here, you won't find it anywhere." The theory of overwhelming display would be the same for any Syms store, no matter where it was. The lowest level was always everything for men, using the same décor and impact that was put in place in the Park Place basement.

The store was just blocks from Wall Street, the New York Stock Exchange, the Woolworth Building, and City Hall. It was near both the Hudson Tubes, running trains between Manhattan and New Jersey, and the Staten Island Ferry, taking office workers home past the Statue of Liberty and Ellis Island. The men in those buildings were Sy's customers.

More business meant he was able to expand his offerings, and that meant more careful cultivation of the brand manufacturers who were his suppliers. He needed more surplus goods from brand-name makers that he could buy cheaply and still make a profit selling at wholesale or below. Sy and Irving often hung around with the tight community of men's clothing manufacturers at the 1290 Sixth Avenue building, long-since demolished for a modern forty-three-story office building. Their brands included London Fog and Stanley Blacker.

Sy would remain close to the manufacturers, playing tennis nearly every day with groups of them for years. These relationships were the key to his business success, and he never forgot that.

He had taped to the back of his bathroom door inspirational sayings by Dr. Kent M. Keith called Paradoxical Commandments. A few:

If you do good, people will accuse you of selfish ulterior motives. Do good anyway.

The good you do today will be forgotten tomorrow. Do good anyway.

What you spend years building may be destroyed overnight. Build anyway.

Sy and Irving understood the manufacturing calendar and knew when these guys had returns from department stores and had to sell out last season's merchandise. The goal was to get more brands and have a larger offering of merchandise to the customers. Since there were no secrets in the clothing industry, once Sy and Irving's store became a reliable place to get rid of extra merchandise for cash, more manufacturers got interested. Irving had more connections to the suit and coat makers, while Sy knew the haberdashers—makers of underwear and socks and such.

By this time, they had employees to help them with buying. This type of buying was labor-intensive, far more than just making phone calls or later sending faxes back and forth or much, much later ordering online. Someone always needed to run up to a showroom on a moment's notice as the buyer of last resort who had cash. When Gant would call and say, "I've got sixty dozen shirts," one of Sy's guys would run up there. The seller would say, "Take out your pencil and make an offer," and then they'd negotiate a price. Since they knew Sy wouldn't use their names in advertising, they didn't care what price he charged, so he could charge under wholesale— the key to off-price selling.

Sy and Irving stayed in the store at 45 Park Place until 1990. When Sy bought Irving out and moved on to other locations, the Pomerantz family became the owner of 45 Park Place and rented it out to Burlington Coat Factory until Irving's death. Today the building has been redeveloped into a residential tower.

After opening stores in Buffalo and Miami, Sy thought it might be good to sell to customers not just where they worked, but also where they lived. In 1971 he opened the first Syms in the suburbs, on Route 4 in Paramus, New Jersey.

Although we didn't realize it at the time, it changed our business forever.

CHAPTER 3

Branching Out

Men are respectable only as they respect.
—Ralph Waldo Emerson

Gant had called Sy and asked if he'd open stores in Miami in 1969 and Buffalo the next year, mainly to sell their shirts. He also had some swimwear in Miami (and short-sleeve Gant shirts). Both stores depended on the power of the Gant name.

The real expansion didn't come, though, until 1971, when he decided to open his first suburban stores outside of Manhattan, in Paramus and Woodbridge, New Jersey. These stores were soon closed as we moved them to bigger sites nearby. At first, we rented the stores, but as our sales grew, we bought the sites. As Sy said, "Who wants to work for the landlord?"

Until then, Sy didn't really know New Jersey, being New York City through and through. Eventually we'd open forty-five more stores across the country over the next forty or so years.

The New Jersey locations made sense because Sy asked his customers where they lived, and most lived in New Jersey! These stores also allowed women to shop during the week while their spouses were at work, so we added more women's clothes.

There were several other reasons the suburbs made sense. For one, real estate was cheaper and more available, you could have on-site parking, and a lot of retail employees lived closer to the suburban stores than they would have to a city location. Walmart and Kmart pretty much did the same thing.

The locations all shared basic characteristics. They were low-rise, warehouse-like buildings on a major highway, often where it met another major highway. They were close to, but not in, at least one major regional shopping mall, usually in communities of not less than two million people. These were destination stores—you intended to go to Syms, not just run in as an afterthought after shopping at the store next door.

> Expansion brought us some surprises. The Paramus store, in particular, drew a large number of Hasidic Jews as customers, and this proved true in other locations as well. Because they couldn't shop before sundown on Saturday, we kept the Paramus store open until 9 p.m. instead of the normal 7 p.m. closing. Sy said he never really understood why these religious Jews loved the store, but he said he always loved them back. Another sign of respect.

For future locations, we'd put a spot on a map and look for locations no more than a forty-five-minute drive from that spot: For example where Route 50 crossed Route 7 in Falls Church, Virginia. We'd put maps in all our store-opening ads. For the New Jersey stores, you could easily see the location on Route 4, later Route 17. Ads would say: *Thanks to you, we're moving to a larger location to accommodate an enhanced collection of designer and brand-name clothing.*

At these new stores, on suits and overcoats, we would keep the labels on the garments and only snip them out once they were purchased. We'd stick the labels in the bag.

By now, the designers were getting more comfortable dealing with us and we signed up more and more big names, including Brioni, Pierre Cardin, Ralph Lauren.

The basic Syms store exterior was painted white with the Syms name—only those four letters—on the side of the highway that faced the intersection—illuminated—so that only after sunset could you easily see the name on the building. The illuminated lettering was really only visible at night. Sy did this on purpose. He wanted customers to try to find the store. There was nothing to indicate we sold clothing. If you found us, you really wanted to buy a suit or a shirt or a blouse.

Interior walls and ceilings were painted in black matte, with unfinished ceilings revealing naked pipes. (I started out opposing black walls—I thought they were gloomy—but I later became a convert. The walls were completely covered by merchandise anyway, and with the drop-down ceiling lighting, the walls kind of melted away. What you saw was the merchandise. We kept the black walls. I gave up.) We locked all the bathrooms. If a customer needed to go, they could ask their educator to unlock it.

Since the men's suit department had the biggest ticket prices, it was given the—literal—red-carpet treatment. In this department you would find individual, private fitting rooms, each with a door, not a curtain, for privacy. When a man tried on a suit, he came out of the fitting room and stood on the alteration block, where a tailor would come out to tell him if the suit needed more alterations than just the length of the sleeves and the length of the leg. If those were the only alterations needed, our customers had the unique advantage of being able to wait until the alterations were completed. This offering was normally only found in the highest-end men's stores.

It was great theater for the other customers shopping in the department. Onlooking customers often made comments on how well or poorly the person trying on the suit looked. Another factor adding to the drama of the alteration block was the tailor himself (they were all men). Most were immigrants or first-generation Americans. Many learned their craft in the old country and prided themselves on being members of the tailors' union. We were a union company from the start, so this fit right into our culture.

The men's department carpeting was the only flash of color in the stores—besides the merchandise. A fashion publication once described the basic Syms store as "comically depressing: fluorescent lights buzzed overhead as hunchbacked elderly salesmen adjust their toupees and drift listlessly about the racks of clothing." That always gave me a wry chuckle. Customers loved our educators, and as they left with an armful of bargains, they probably didn't find them listless or depressing.

The idea was that not a dime was being spent on frivolous decorations—it was all going to make sure the customer got the best price. (We actually spent quite a bit on custom designed store furniture and the clothing racks that jammed each store.) Even the fitting rooms were basic, with in the early years not even curtains closing them off, to prevent theft. What the customer saw when entering was clothes literally everywhere, practically floor to ceiling, and a well-dressed, smiling educator waiting to answer their questions and help them through the selection and fitting process.

Given my dad's background in broadcasting, he always made sure each store had a state-of-the art public address system. Unlike many retailers of the time, who played background elevator music to create a relaxed mood, he used this system to broadcast three different forty-five-second announcements every hour. Starting in 1969 at Park Place, these were done live by Sy, standing in the middle of the store, microphone in hand, or by the store manager if Sy wasn't there. We later recorded them. I used to write them and it was pretty hard to make them sound fresh. "Did you know every garment must bear a label showing its fiber content?"

A bit later, the suburban store managers would add live announcements, including "dividend" announcements. These were special prices only available in-store for limited periods of time. Eventually we offered dividends every day from 5 p.m. to 6 p.m. Monday through Friday. We'd pick one item from each department: "In our women's blouse department, Anne Klein nationally advertised blouse $50, Syms off-price $29.99, from 5 to 6, $10 off." This was great word of mouth—people came for these hours to try to catch an even bigger bargain.

With the advent of the women's department, Syms found its biggest single seller, which would remain true throughout our existence: pantyhose. At the beginning Sy could pick up millions of pairs for $1 and sell them all for $1.25. Over the years the prices changed, but at least the 25 percent margin didn't.

Apart from these dividends, Syms never had "sales" as such, because our everyday prices were low and as we'll see later, they even went down as the merchandise grew older. But from the earliest days in lower Manhattan, Sy ran what he called "Bashes": twice a year, in February for Presidents' Day, and end of summer on Labor Day.

At first it was by handwritten invitation only—people would sign up in the store if they wanted to be invited to Bash. (The store would be closed to the public for two days, and only admit people who could show the invitation card. This caused quite a stir and was one of the elements that caused Bash to grow. Of course, if you made it into the store, you got the sale price and then told all your friends.) We eventually developed a mailing list for these Bashes, which topped out at more than 500,000 names. Customers wanted to be sure they weren't excluded from the next Bash.

During Bash, a customer would walk into the store and hear announcements and see signs that showed dividends in almost all merchandise, with the deepest dividends on merchandise we wanted to clear out to make room for the new season inventory. A $500 nationally advertised Bill Blass suit, Syms everyday $299, would be $249, or if we needed to clear it out, $199. Everything was marked down, our dividend. At full maturity, Bashes got to be ten days long twice a year.

I loved when a mom and her pack of kids walked out the stores with arms full of bags of clothes that would see the family through for at least the next six months, maybe until the next Bash. It meant much more to me than just sales we rang up on the registers.

It meant we were helping people, and to do so required a special kind of team.

When someone was hired, they were given a three-week training period, where they would be trained in each department, understanding the name brands and designers we carried, how we cared for the items, what we expected the educators to tell our customers, how to care for the merchandise (a lot of practice folding and rehanging) and understanding what's in the inventory number (later barcode), which was the merchandise's birthmark from the moment it came into our distribution center until the moment it left with the customer. We wanted our coworkers to understand the full life of each item so they could explain it to customers, as well as judging if that garment was going to be right for that customer.

They would work in the receiving room, they would work in the fitting room, they would work at the register. This made it possible for the coworker to learn how to be a valuable addition to the team in the store. No coworker had just one job, except the tailors and the men's educators. This also enabled the coworkers to see where their interest and talents lay. If someone really liked working the register, they could stay there, or they could transfer to where they wanted to go. Educators would learn about themselves.

We really spent a lot of time on this. I made countless training visits and presentations. It was that important. Sy and I made a thirty-five-minute-long training tape in 1990 that was sent to every store manager to be shared with all the coworkers. For most of it, Sy is talking straight into the camera, just like for our TV commercials, intoning rules and tips for the men's department, the shoe department, and most important, he says, the cash register and the customer service desk. Managers would use this tape to reinforce everything they had already told the coworkers. The whole business ran on fanatic attention to detail.

We start at men's suits, pointing out the vast selection, which educators should emphasize. "We have more than four hundred suits." Sy goes over the rules for alterations and explains why we need to charge a nominal fee—which, by the way, was the same for women.

Standing next to a register, Sy says a pleasant, lucrative store visit can all come undone if the cashier is nasty, slow, unpleasant or argumentative. Keep everything as easy as possible. Smile and say thank you.

All our registers had a back store on the wall behind the register where we displayed a few impulse items such as perfume and garment bags. Sy didn't want the cashiers spending time selling while lines formed in front of their registers. A customer should say: Give me one of these, Sy says. He spends a lot of time on how to fold a garment bag to store it. No detail is too small. Every sight and sound makes an experience.

"Everything has to be quick here. The most important thing is accuracy and the second is your attitude. Be professional. Always pick the proper-sized bag for an item." He demonstrates how to hold a bag open and not have stuff flopping around in too big a bag. We had bags for one shirt, three shirts, bigger items and much bigger items, all within easy reach under the counter.

The second most important area, Sy says, is the consumer desk. Coworkers there must be courteous no matter what the situation and resolve any issues, sending the customer away quickly and smiling. It should be a happy experience. Make them feel good regardless. "If that customer doesn't come back, you might not be working."

Moving to the children's section, he delivers a detailed theory on how to display infants' and toddlers' clothes on upper and lower racks, including how many of each style and size should go where on each of the racks. He repeats this demonstration for ladies' sweaters and blouses, in mind-numbing detail on how to have an even spread of sizes and labels across the shelves. Again, no detail is too small. At one point he says that if a customer sees three of the same item hanging next to each other with the same color tag, they might decide the item isn't selling and will wait for the automatic price reduction. Spread them among the other items.

In the children's department, there is an extensive discussion of the one to four theory, which dictates how managers should display items on the double hanging racks. If they've got two of the same, put one up and one down.

For women, theory dictates how to group sizes and what proportion displayed should be size 12 or 14 or 16. It's all very scientific and I'll spare you further details of this theory, but it worked.

Sy loved rules and we put a lot of them in the coworker manuals we gave everybody. One of the last editions, in 2010, had the 10 Rules of Customer Service and how to display and enforce them. They are all based on respecting the customer's time and respecting them as individuals. Not only did I write some of these rules, I embraced them all.

Here are the rules:

1. Treat every customer with the respect you yourself expect to receive. They are the reason we stay in business. (Note: Respect is rule number one, sort of like the First Amendment.)

2. Greet each customer with a smile, direct eye contact, and a good morning, afternoon or evening as soon as they enter our store. Your expression, body stance, and tone of voice should say, "Welcome, we're glad you came to shop."

3. Determine the customer's need once you've said hello.

4. If a customer requests a certain item or specific size, never point or give directions; escort the customer to the proper area.

5. Always look up while doing stock to say hello to shoppers in your area. Smile to show that you are available for any questions they might have.

6. Be aware of suggestive selling opportunities. Let the customer know we have tops to match the bottoms they've selected. Escort them to the tops and excuse yourself to let them look through the merchandise.

7. Be knowledgeable about the various brand names, fiber contents, and sizes throughout your area.

8. Remember to remain cool and levelheaded. Be extra-kind and respectful to customers. Management presence is of the utmost importance.

9. Help a customer with a zipper or the buttons on the back of an outfit in the dressing room.

10. Be honest to customers. If the suit doesn't fit, suggest another manufacturer or size; don't tell the customer what you think he/she wants to hear.

Store managers were to go over these rules with employees on a regular basis, as well as post them in break rooms and on message boards.

Managers and coworkers violated these rules at their peril, and actually hardly ever did. They worked. We built our business together and everyone thrived.

Everything from the interior walls and ceilings and size and color and content of the price tags to the positioning of the shelves and racks to the placement of items, merchandise we needed to move up front, more expensive pieces in the back, to the patter of the educators to the simplicity of the checkout, was designed to make it easy to buy. Years later Sy would reflect that he wanted the customer to feel they were getting a bargain without his having to shout at them. The customer should leave the store feeling they had gotten a bargain.

Which they had.

Meanwhile, the retailing world was changing with incredible speed and we needed to adapt, and did so with mixed success.

The 1960s was an amazing decade. It saw nationwide protests over the Vietnam War, the rise of the women's movement, Americans walking on the moon, the growth of television as the dominant medium, and in my world, a burst of creativity and new technology that changed how clothing was designed, manufactured, and sold.

My father was very sensitive to the environment changing right around the time he broke with his brother and started his own shop. He always said you had to have a good idea, but you also needed to know how to structure something to support that idea. His structure came from the burst in manufacturing and creativity of American clothing designers, such as Ralph Lauren, Bill Blass, and Donna Karan establishing fresh name brands that denoted quality. This was the start of the enormous investment and attention to names and labels that became our lifeblood.

We later did introduce a house label, called "SSS" and denoted in the garment with an SSS brand. We put it on some men's suits and ladies' blouses where he had acquired quality fabric and could order as many pieces as we wished. This provided a cushion against running out of, say, white blouses. However, many Ralph Lauren blouses we got sold out in a day!

Sy knew he had to find other ways to help out manufacturers, to remain vital for them to do business with him. He would go to a Ralph Lauren and say, "Don't worry about any overproduction. We'll take whatever you've got left over and we'll pay cash." He also again assured them he wouldn't use their name in advertising so as to not compete with their brand. Repeated over many hundreds of manufacturers, this assured us of a constant supply of product, and then a healthier bottom line.

This was a classic confluence of interests—one hand feeding the other. The success of this model encouraged dozens of new brands to enter the market, not all of which made it. As they established the value proposition associated with their name, start-ups could be reassured that once they had a few seasons under their belts, they would be able to make bolder production decisions at the beginning of each season, because they knew Sy would take any excess off their hands. Because we never returned anything, we told them we'll find the price we can sell it for, so we need to get the best price from you.

There are few win-wins in life, but this was one of them.

Sy's confidence in this model inspired confidence in the manufacturers once they saw it work. They loved us. We grew up with them in sixties, seventies, and beginning of the eighties. Early on the market was pretty boring, with just a few brands. Then there was a sudden burst of investment and energy that went hand in hand with the explosion of the suburbs and the malls that served them. We were lucky to be right there with the knowledge and cash to help all these creators. Sy used to say: "Never forget how important luck is in any outcome."

Luck and trust. Trust was a big part of our success. Trust is what gets you over the ebbs and flows of time and business. We were very trusted, not just because Sy and I were visible as family owners—manufacturers and customers always knew who to go to with a complaint—but also because we never did bait and switch. We never told a brand or a customer something and they then found something different in the store. Trust takes a very long time to build, but it can disappear very quickly.

We always strove to tell the customer more than they thought they wanted to know. We felt we could never go wrong sharing information. This was the culture of our company, and it was the same outside the store during buying negotiations or on our TV commercials as it was inside the store as an educator made a sale. If you try to have an inside and outside culture, people will soon find out. You're inviting people into your store with the same intimacy involved in inviting them into your home. If there is something fishy going on, they can feel it.

All of these things became apparent to me as I got more involved with the company.

CHAPTER 4
Getting Started at Syms

*The best protector any woman can have, one that will serve
her at all times and in all places, is courage.*
—Elizabeth Cady Stanton

While growing up, I had worked only one summer at a Syms store. It never occurred to me that I would want to work there permanently or make it my life's vocation. I progressed through adolescence and young adulthood following my own interests. I went to Finch College, majoring in English, and later earned an MS in communications at Boston University.

The fifteen months in 1974 and 1975 that I spent living on Ware Street in Cambridge, taking the red line to Commonwealth Avenue for classes at the College of Communication, were some of the most exciting months of my intellectual life. For the first time in my career as a student, I really had to learn and use collaborative skills to complete work, and the effort was transformative. I was charged up all the time with ideas and possibilities.

The time I spent at Boston University was a launching pad for my self-confidence as a manager of change, and I was hungry for change. I had the opportunity to learn that change can only happen when others are convinced that they will benefit from the outcome and see themselves as change agents too. With that energy and positive attitude, I started my career in broadcasting and soon after, joined my dad at Syms in his store in lower Manhattan.

After school I got a job as a paralegal for Maurice Nadjari, a New York State special prosecutor, whose job came into existence by state decree after corruption was exposed in the police department in the Serpico case, immortalized in the movie by Al Pacino. But ever my father's daughter, I also leaned toward entertainment, first as an assistant to Peter Straus, then president of WMCA, a radio station in New York City, and then as an associate producer of a live daily midday talk show. It turns out associate producers are expendable, and when a new boss replaced Peter, I got caught up in a cost-cutting campaign and was out. I had to find something else to do.

This was a traumatic experience for me—what did I do wrong?—but one I learned from. I often tell student audiences that while getting fired for whatever reason is terrible, it's a chance to clear your mind and try to figure out what you really want to do. The cliché that getting fired can be the best thing that could happen isn't wrong.

I got some freelance work and had dinner with my dad every few weeks. During one of these get-togethers in 1977, he told me that he and his right-hand person, who acted as his sounding board, were thinking of expanding, and perhaps would choose a market outside the New York area.

I always felt my father's excitement when he talked about Syms. He did it a lot and sometimes, like any child, I resented his talking about the business so much because it would push other things out of the conversation. But in retrospect, I got an understanding of the business and what it takes to start a company. I felt his excitement, the energy, and the good time he was having as part of this experience. Sy always believed in what he was doing and how he was doing it, regardless of something taking longer than expected coming to fruition. His determination gave him complete confidence in his ability to make the right decision. That was very seductive—you can't seduce anyone while having a bad time, and Sy rarely had a down day.

I think it's also important to come into the family business with a certain skill. I came to Syms with expertise in media planning. Media planning is deciding how to place the company's ads—whether they should be on television, radio, in newspapers, or social media—and how the mix should be in terms of time, frequency and channels.

When I was at WNEW as an assistant producer, I noticed that people working for big rep agencies seemed to make a lot of money. They didn't work very hard and they had three-hour lunches. What could be better? So, I took a course and began moonlighting as a media planner. Now, as anyone who has ever worked in television production knows, cutbacks happen frequently, and I lost my job. But I was able to work as a freelance media planner while I thought about what I might do next.

Almost a year later, my dad was planning the opening of the first Syms store outside of the New York metropolitan area, whose location was chosen through research. I suggested that I work on a part-time basis and put together the media plan for Syms entering the new market. I knew it was in his head that it would be nice to have Marcy part of the company in some way. I wasn't sure the way, but I knew that I couldn't just go into Syms as Sy's daughter.

First of all, the company wasn't big enough for that. And more importantly, my coming in just as Sy's daughter would alienate everyone else who thought they could grow with the company. I knew I had to contribute something and when I figured out what I could do, what I had more expertise in than anyone else, the timing was right.

Sy had found a community that was cushioned on both

sides by two of the highest per-capita income markets in the United States. It was the Washington, DC, area, and the site for this new Syms store would be in Falls Church, Virginia.

With no full-time job at the time, it seemed natural for me to offer to go to Washington and work with him on preparing an advertising and media plan. Syms had been a TV advertiser since 1974, and Sy carefully educated me on his successful use of the medium. I researched the Washington area, and after four weeks proposed a buying schedule for the local media.

My father gave me a budget. He told me what his ideas were. For a couple of weeks, I sat in my hotel room just watching TV and listening to radio and reading newspapers. I came out with a fairly good idea about what we could do, which complemented our form of advertising.

Sy and I worked on a TV, radio, and print media plan for Falls Church in March 1978. This included full-page newspaper ads, which I wrote, which featured a map showing our location right where Route 50 crossed Route 7, as well as radio and TV commercials that started three weeks before the opening. Since Sy felt, correctly, that we could get a better deal on ads that ran for longer, we took out yearlong contracts. This was a big investment for us but appreciated by our media partners. It became standard practice for us.

Living in a DC-area motel, helping hire and train people, taught me a lot. So did all those dinners with Dad. The more involved I got, the more energized I got. My job as media and marketing manager became anything that needed to be done, including ordering lunch or setting up chairs for meetings or calling the police to get rid of illegal parkers in our parking lot, or increasingly, meeting with contractors as we built out the store.

From the first, I loved store openings. Preparing for them was akin to preparing a Broadway show. I was absorbed and inspired by numbers of balls in the air, with me being responsible for them all landing in the right place at the right time. Besides the advertising and media coverage, I was hiring people, making sure the racks and shelves were in the right places, overseeing signage, and pretty much everything else.

Sy would come down from New York once a week, stay all day and go back. His visits were the glue that kept everything together. His vision was solid, his leadership sure-footed, and his energy infectious. He would tell stories of the old days in order to infuse the staff with the history of the company. Sometimes he'd buy everyone lunch. We were creating one big family.

This 45,000-foot store, our largest in the suburbs at that time, needed two overall managers as well as department managers. We transferred a few of our best from New York and New Jersey stores so we'd be confident they would administer our values and store experiences. Syms was different from other store experiences and you did need training.

I signed up to work as a contractor from January 1 until the store opening, a three-month deal. I officially became a Syms employee at the Falls Church opening, but well before that I knew I was going to throw my hat in for a full-time job.

For those three months I read newspapers, listened to the radio, watched TV, and drove around town. I met with the few buyers we had who'd come down from New York and we'd do old-fashioned market research. We'd drive around to department stores to see which brands were prominently displayed in stores within a thirty-minute radius. It helped us tell manufacturers which brands they might want to sell at this new venture. We also noted when predominately men or predominantly women, or predominantly couples, were shopping and what for. Today you can just plug numbers into an algorithm, but then it was something you had to figure out and analyze, then adjust your plans.

Setting up the Falls Church store was a collaborative exercise and one I was happy to repeat many times over as we ex-

panded. I always loved store openings because they generated the same type of excitement as right before you go live
on a TV or radio show. You need to be alive and alert and on
top of your game.

Because it was my first, Falls Church was probably the
most fun. I was the boss's daughter, but that never came up.
I didn't presume to give orders and was just part of a team.
I did whatever someone said needed to be done, and I
never stopped learning. I had experience and wasn't a
show-off. It was all very natural and organic, not at all pre-
ordained. No one was threatened by me: They knew I was
running media and I'd sink or swim based on how successful our opening was.

Falls Church was a prototype for all our future suburban
stores. It was on two levels, with the men's store a self-
contained unit on the first floor. When you came in, your
eyes were met by racks upon racks of men's suits and sports
coats.

Among the hundreds of planning details we had worked
on, we had interviewed several local policemen before we
asked one to be our opening day security guard. We wanted
somebody with a personality that made them unseen but
present. No detail was too small!

> We always opened on a Thursday because you could
> crescendo into the weekend, when men would shop.
> Men were our core customers for our highest margin
> suits and overcoats. They showed up after 5 p.m. and on
> weekends.

At Falls Church, like every store we opened, Sy would
post a dollar bill with the end torn off on the company bulletin
board in the back of the store. That's because his mother-in-

law, Clara Glickman—who called him Son, and he called her Mom—had given him such a bill as a good luck charm for his very first store. It was one of our few superstitions.

Back then, all white-collar workers wore suits and ties to the office every day and they needed a wardrobe. We wanted to satisfy those needs. As more women entered the workforce, they too dressed for their careers. Our women's departments reflected those needs.

For both sexes, this was heavy-duty suit time. Think Ronald and Nancy Reagan. Or Jimmy and Rosalyn Carter. During his presidency, which coincided with the Falls Church opening, all the Carters—including his mother, Miss Lillian—came in to shop.

One Christmas we had for sale lots of goofy holiday sweaters, and we were selling them at crazy low prices. I remember seeing Miss Lillian with an armful of gift sweaters and a big smile on her face.

Other retailers would do soft openings, with no ads, just to check that all systems were working ahead of a big launch later on. Sy never liked that idea. He liked the pressure of having to show up at showtime. We advertised every opening. When doors opened, everyone had to give 100 percent effort. This wasn't a rehearsal. It was all done in real time.

We learned one thing from this opening that we eventually changed in all of our stores. Normally, we wouldn't hold merchandise for customers. If you wanted it, you had to buy it right then and if you didn't, you took the chance it might be gone when you came back. But so many women in Falls Church asked us to hold suits until their husbands could come try them on that we changed the policy on the spot. We'd hold the item until the evening so they could come back with their husbands. We responded to conditions and made changes appropriately.

We didn't accept national credit cards until 1997. You could pay by cash, check, or our own Syms credit card. I tried for years to change this. Sy's reason was he thought this policy reinforced in the customer's mind that this was an opportune moment to find that garment at that price and you have to have the money to pay for it. We weren't selling on installments. Besides, why should we pay the credit card company fees?

I finally got him to relent when I could show him that the cash that was lost on bad checks was pretty much equal to the credit card company charges. We traded bad checks for credit card fees. Still, if you had a Syms card you could get refunds on returns. If you used another credit card, we gave only a store credit.

Opening day at Falls Church was a blowout success.

While our off-duty policeman quietly kept order in the very crowded parking lot, a crowd of almost all women gathered outside the front door. When the doors opened at 10 a.m., we had women rushing in with strollers, mothers and teenaged daughters, friends on shopping dates. They mobbed the second-floor women's department, but also checked out the men's department because they would often tell their husbands and boyfriends where to shop. Our educators made sure they were welcome to bring their partners back any time.

Boy, did they. The first Saturday we needed more cops (called by our off-duty cop) in the parking lot because it was so crowded that traffic was backed up on both Routes 7 and 50. Both at Falls Church and elsewhere, the town eventually installed traffic lights to enable better entry into our lot. We even got local TV and radio coverage because of the traffic jams! This was another benefit of three months' preparation. I knew people at all four local TV stations and twenty AM and FM radio stations, because I had negotiated the advertising contracts. Many of them saw our opening as a great news story. We got tons of free publicity. Everything we hoped to happen, did.

The opening was another confirmation of Sy's early insight about our advertising being aspirational because our offer to our customers was aspirational. At Falls Church and our other suburban stores, on a typical Saturday you'd see more Cadillacs and Mercedes in our lots than in the department store lots down the road. Aspirational people wanted great clothes but didn't want to pay full price. These were our people.

We were announcing store opening thank-you dividends—$10 off Gant shirts for the next two hours—on the PA system, which meant dollars off in every department for the first few days after the opening. Again, only available in the store. The ladies rushed home to bring their men. Don't forget there was no online at that time. (In the early 2000s we experimented with online but it didn't work for us. It seemed confusing and didn't enhance our core business. We always felt the sense of a bargain was an inherent advantage in our stores.)

One of the unique factors we wanted people to understand was the sliding price scale on our price tags only for women's clothing. It was a way to create excitement and make the consumer feel they'd better buy it now while they had it in their hands. In addition, it was in keeping with Sy's philosophy that we were in the business for the manufacturer and the designer, and they benefited from us moving the goods and buying more from them.

But it also showed our main vulnerability, as designers eventually opened their own outlet stores and became more vertical retailers. They then controlled their own merchandise and didn't need us.

A dress might be nationally advertised at $60, but be $39 at Syms. The date the dress hit the floor was noted. After ten days that price would go down to $32, after twenty days to $25, and be finally marked at $19 after thirty days on the floor. After another thirty days we'd move the item to a special display rack. We'd keep track. If we had a whole lot of stuff on that rack from the same buyer, that buyer might have to go.

We trained our educators to explain this, but it still was a little difficult for many shoppers to get their heads around. They sometimes wanted the final price no matter how long the item had been around.

This was kind of *Let's Make a Deal*, but with the whole deal in front of you. You could buy today or come back after ten or twenty days and hope the item was still there. (We even had people roll up dresses or blouses and tuck them away behind displays or in dressing rooms, hoping we wouldn't find them. We usually did.) In any event, making people develop a buying strategy was a great way to engage them.

While the Falls Church store was run by the general manager, not by me, working there gave me, for the first time, the exciting feeling that any addicted entrepreneur gets hooked on: the excitement, energy, momentum, and the feeling you're part of something that's going to be terrific. We were providing customers with something they couldn't find anywhere else.

After the opening weekend at Falls Church, we all came back to earth. Retail is a day-to-day grind. We had to stay on top of our inventory constantly, because in our business if something was out of stock in a certain color or size, we lost the sale. We couldn't promise to get a specific item in because we never knew if we could. Customers wouldn't forgive us if we didn't have what they wanted. They'd go somewhere else and it was hard to get them to come back after they had made the long drive to our store.

At the store opening I told Sy I loved being part of it and wanted to work for the company and was willing to do anything he needed me to do. Back in New York, I was put in charge of media, training, and customer relations, reporting directly to Sy, but needing to engage with all the other people he had in top management. The challenge for me was to win over all the people who had helped Sy grow from one store in lower Manhattan to other markets. It was all "show me you can do it." They didn't give me the benefit of the doubt, and rightly so. Just like anywhere else.

After coming back to New York, I asked my father if he thought I did a good job. He said yes. Then I said I would like to try working at Syms full-time. I wanted to set up a media department and I was willing to do anything else that was needed. I also asked him to constantly give me feedback so that I knew how I was doing. By asking for that, I was letting him know that while this was a career move that was important to me, I would be constantly reevaluating and I expected him to evaluate me as well.

When I made the commitment, I decided that it was on me to get some hardcore education about what we were selling, I went to a night class on textiles at the Fashion Institute of Technology. The teacher knew about decorative textiles, not clothing; drapes and upholstery and such, not really about suits or dress fabrics. But he had a great knowledge about supply chains that was very valuable to me. He became a nice sounding board for me in those early years. It was a classic case of needing a mentor and how important that could be. At different stages in your career you need an independent voice, most usefully someone with experience broader than your own.

A class called retail math at FIT helped a lot. Sy did all the math in his head and was almost never wrong. He thought in dozens, a neat trick, learned as a buyer for George long ago. He could look at a wall and see it with six shelves and envision to the garment how many dozen shirts would fit in 30 feet, 60 feet, or 120 feet. Despite FIT's best efforts, Sy's natural affinity for math relationships turned out to be nontransferable!

Entering the family business was not a decision I made

lightly. I knew that everyone's eyes would be on me and that I couldn't just float in and float out in twelve months. If I did that, my father would lose respect for me, and I would lose respect for myself. So, I really had to make a commitment and I decided to give myself five years.

Running a media department wasn't a full-time job at Syms. We did our media buys for a twelve-month period for both TV and radio. I'd spend about three months preparing and doing heavy negotiations, and then spend the rest of the year monitoring. I had a lot of time to be the switchboard operator, the receptionist, and act as secretary to my dad.

I became familiar with my dad's style of management and I saw where and how my job could develop. Because I was the switchboard operator, I got the customer calls. I started doing the customer relations, which was basically resolving problems. That got me in touch with store managers. I also took the minutes of the monthly manager meetings my dad held. I don't take shorthand, but I do write pretty fast. By keeping the minutes of those meetings and disseminating them to store managers, I gradually became somewhat of the communications person with the managers on points that were discussed at meetings.

I was not authorized to give answers, and I did so anyway. But—and this is a big *but*—I asked a lot of questions to make sure I had the right answers to give.

After about two years, I asked my dad if I could learn something about buying because, after all, we sell clothing. I had been taking courses at night at FIT to learn textile science and retail accounting. I started going out with some of the buyers to learn the various markets, from haberdashery to ladies' wear.

In the meantime, I got involved in real estate and site selection. It's something that I'm still very actively involved in, and it's one of my favorite facets of the business. Part of my training in media buying was understanding demographics, so I had the background for understanding the demographics for real estate.

In March of 1978, I was ready to make the kind of commitment to Syms that I probably could not have made before. I think the company and I were ready for each other.

First, Syms could expand. The off-price apparel business had potential for growth in many markets and Sy was willing to try new markets as long as his existing stores remained profitable.

Having held several jobs, I knew what the work world was like. I knew about the long hours, the lack of recognition for women, and the uncertainty of job security.

The company could use my experience and skills.

My self-confidence was high. I was pretty certain that I could master any techniques that I needed. After all, I had been familiar with the business through osmosis since childhood.

The future of the company meant a lot to me, for both financial and personal reasons. I was very fond of my father and admired him tremendously.

I wanted to help him and I thought I could learn more from him.

CHAPTER 5

Down to Work

Management is doing things right; leadership is doing the right things.
—Peter Drucker

When I got into management, I came in on the coattails of a lot of women who were already breaking barriers. The hardest part for me, besides being the only woman in the room, was that I was also the daughter of the chairman, Sy Syms.

I found that there was an assumption that I might not have earned the seat I occupied. At least I *thought* I knew what they were thinking. In the beginning, I was insecure about that. I tried to show them how smart I was. If someone suggested something, I would say, "I heard about that," and tell them all I knew, even if I didn't totally understand it. But you only have to make a silly or foolish comment once to start to change your behavior. I'd have to say it took three to five years to get beyond that.

If I learned anything over the years, it's that it is not necessary to show someone how smart you are. It will come across in the process of developing a business relationship. When I became less insecure about myself, I didn't try as hard. What I would say, with certainty and with a good deal of experience, is that you do get to use everything you learn. No training or experience, good or bad, needs to be wasted.

At 45 Park Place my desk was right outside Sy's office. All the complaints came to me. Sitting where I did, I saw all of his visitors come in, and I was often asked to join the meetings.

When I first joined the company in 1978, we did a five-year plan. This became a point of discussion and review and comparison with what Sy saw was needed next. Once we had something pretty well put together, there was no need to constantly ask: What happens next? We had the overall direction—we just needed to make sure that if something unexpected came up, we could react. We made a new plan after we went public.

Those first five years were about building a more solid foundation for growth, including hiring more professionals and setting up a more organizational structure, where it wasn't just a couple of talented people doing all the jobs. This is the key point where many family-owned businesses succeed, fail, or just back off in the face of the challenges.

In order to succeed, you need to understand people. What motivates them? How do you organize them without suffocating them in bureaucracy? Who has leadership skills? There are lots of how-to books out there, but nothing is like actually trying to do it in real time as the stores are operating.

For me, it meant understanding more about my dad's leadership and how I could enhance his strengths and minimize his deficits. He was really strong in messaging and vision and never got tired of telling people his plans and what our limits were, because of the limited supply of designer and brand names.

Dealing with the outside was a different story. Sy wasn't operational. He knew when outcomes were wrong, but he was not necessarily interested in the minutia in trying to correct them. I saw an opportunity to get involved in operations—everything from insuring we opened on time with enough personnel, to changing the clocks for daylight saving time, to buying and maintaining the machinery at the distribution center, to dealing with the unions, to parking security. We were an excellent team! We sometimes used this difference in talents and skills in the good cop, bad cop scenario when negotiating.

It was important to get all this right because we wanted to use it all as a template for further expansion. In principle, we wanted the shopping experience to be the same in all Syms stores.

We had to train specially because our customers were different. Do you ever get in Diane von Furstenberg blouses? We wouldn't know until we made the visit to the von Furstenberg showroom if there would be merchandise for us. Our customers were confident shoppers—especially the men. They knew exactly what they were looking for and would often go to a department store first to see what the new looks were, and then see if they could find it cheaper at Syms. They almost always could.

One thing I learned early on: At Syms we had to make sure everyone came to work properly dressed! Some of our younger coworkers didn't have appropriate clothes. We gave them a wardrobe allowance and we sold them our stuff at cost, using this allowance. Our dress code required a jacket and tie and slacks at least for men and similar business dress for women. Since we were promoting career dressing for our customers, our coworkers had to dress like that as well. We later adapted to casual Fridays for both customers and staff by stocking more denim—Lee jeans—and more casual shirts. We encouraged our staff to buy from their employer, but if they didn't want to, they could go somewhere else, but without the allowance.

The clothes were just the start. Personal hygiene is a delicate workplace issue, but we couldn't have coworkers with bad breath dealing with customers, and visible dandruff on a dark suit is a bad look in a clothing store. Managers needed to be sensitive—helpful, not scolding, and never personal. But grooming issues had to be addressed.

You only get one chance to make a good first impression, and both management and the workforce had to be aware of this. We tend to size people up in the first fifteen seconds after we meet them. I had resisted this notion when I was looking for work, but came to see how true it is once I started hiring people. The same goes for the employee-customer relationship. Your credibility comes from the whole package, from the smile down to the shoeshine. Besides, who wants to buy clothes from a sloppy dresser?

As I told Judith Briles for her book *The Confidence Factor* (MasterMedia, 1990), "It's important for all of us to feel comfortable about our own physical package. It doesn't mean that you are beautiful, but merely that you do the best with what you've got—you put together your best outfit, you exercise, you wash your hair, you know that your teeth are clean. All the basics that lead up to when you walk into a room. You don't want to draw attention to yourself in any negative way."

I was always big on hands-on hiring, especially because we needed our people transmitting our message—more so than, say, an average department store. This made hiring particularly important, and over the years I developed a technique useful not just at Syms, but at any profit-making or nonprofit organization or political, charitable or social organization.

I'd meet candidates and see the interview as information gathering by me. It wasn't a chance for them to find out about the company. I'd prepare at least ten questions. These were not "What do you expect to be doing five years from now?"

Rather, they were more like: "If you could relate to me the one time you felt most embarrassed in front of your manager?"

"Why did that occur?"

"What kind of people rub you the wrong way?"

"Describe your perfect boss."

"Who has been a role model for you and what advice did they give you that you still use?"

"If you were part of a team, what would you be doing more than the other members of the team and what would it take for you to be the team leader?"

At the end of the interview, I never shared anything. I would say: "I'm giving you an assignment and if that's satisfied, I'll call you back for a second interview, and you can ask all the questions you want."

The assignment:

Please think of eight questions you need to have answered to your satisfaction for you to accept a job at Syms. These are your questions. Think of what's most important to you."

I'd evaluate these questions as follows:

How many out of the eight are self-serving, selfish, or brown-nosing.

The worst was selfish. "How soon do you get a raise after promotion? Are evaluations connected directly to salary? If I get a complimentary letter from a customer, what kind of recognition do I get?"

Anyone with two or more selfish questions wouldn't get a second interview. And sometimes even one, based on other questions.

I was looking for questions that showed a candidate did research or visited a store. I was turned off if they asked questions about store layout, lighting, or décor, when all they had to do was visit a store.

I wanted to know how they were tuned into an organization. What kind of meetings do you have to keep up effective communication? What kind of training do you offer? How will I be able to train and what additional training tools will I receive to make sure my team is well informed? Are there ways my feedback can be seen to make a difference? What kind of communications will I get about new season products? Can we make merchandising decisions and reorder our own merchandise?

I wanted managers focused on operations. These questions would tell me what would make them successful.

It never failed. Eight out of eight good questions got hired. Sometimes six or seven.

We believed that if someone had the personality and skills for selling and managing, it didn't matter if it was clothing or accessories or whether they came from Lowe's or Men's Wearhouse. We needed strength, energy, and the stamina to walk a store, and above all liking people. They could come from a plumbing supply store and learn they loved fashion. Working with people was key to success at working at a Syms store.

Selling on our floor was different. It really was educating.

"Did you know you can get a $25 Gant shirt for $11.88?" These were great conversation openers, but vital because while a new customer might have seen an ad before coming in, they wouldn't have gotten this specific message.

As with any employer, compensation was always a tricky matter. No matter what you do, you can't pay everyone the same and some people are going to be unhappy. Still, it's important, though often difficult, to treat all your employees the same, or at least transparently fairly. Our unions protected various rights, but we set the hourly and weekly wages. We never paid commissions, since we viewed sales as a team effort.

Years back, a group of young men had joined us and eventually moved into upper management. One of them, who had become a top buyer, left and opened his own store in lower Manhattan, not far from our Trinity Place store. It was lost on nobody that this is what Sy had done decades before when he left his father and brother's store.

He went to the manufacturers and tried to make similar

deals to ours. Given the gossipy nature of the fashion world, we found out almost instantly. As hurt as Sy was, it just reinforced his attitude that this guy was a talented entrepreneur, pursuing his own vision. Sy decided to help him with advice and a small investment. After five years he came back to Syms and Sy gave him an employment contract, which we had never done. Sy knew he wouldn't come back without some guarantee of income. This had a ripple effect throughout the management team. Remember: There are no secrets in retail. They all asked: Where's mine?

We'd always told them that their ability to earn was irrespective of what was happening to the right and left of them. But now everyone started sharing details of their income and bonuses. There was some disparity, though not a lot. Some of this was caused by past earnings history and local cost of living and employment market issues. New York area salaries tended to be higher.

My first major project was our new distribution center in Lyndhurst, New Jersey. Prior to this, each store had to order and store its inventory in whatever space they could find in the store. This was costly and inefficient. We needed a big space.

Once the idea was hatched and Sy had articulated the framework, he was able to delegate. It was left to me to get it done. How do you organize a distribution center? How to flow trucks in and out? Where should it be? How big? Nowadays, you could use the Amazon distribution centers that dot the country as a template. But this was all pre-Amazon.

We worked with a great young woman at Kidder, Peabody to apply for, and get, New Jersey development bonds to help finance the project. We wound up with 8,000 square feet of office space and 90,000 square feet of storage and distribution space.

Once the distribution center opened, we planned our offices. Instead of sitting outside Sy's office as at Park Place, we now had same-size offices, with doors, next to each other. He was fine with that.

These first five years established the foundations for future growth.

I was proud to help, especially in the growth of our women's business.

The first women's department started in Paramus, in answer to Sy's question of Who's going to shop during the day in the suburbs? We started talking to our men's designers and manufacturers who also produced women's clothes. Or they introduced us to women's manufacturers and designers. It turned out that they too had excess inventory they were happy to unload for cash at the end of each season. For a time we had the biggest selection of men's and women's London Fog raincoats in the country.

The women's and men's departments were ideally located on two separate floors. At all suburban stores, to the right would be a glass vestibule, after which was eventually a luggage department. We started this because we found we were becoming a destination for tourists, who sometimes would buy suitcases in which to take home their purchases. Once again, we always tried to understand our customers and give them what they wanted. We later added gift items and infant and children's departments, all of them in the same place in each store and never moving. We wanted customers to know where everything they needed would be, in respect for their time. Women might have forty minutes during their lunch hour or before they needed to pick the kids up from school. It was all about respect.

Clothing for women was separated into career, weekend wear, workout clothes, evening wear, cocktail dresses, pantsuits, seasonal items like sweaters and bathing suits, and lingerie and sleepwear.

Once we got a consistent flow of merchandise from vendors, we were happy to add hard goods like electric blankets, comforters, and shower curtains. We called this section Domestic and the goods often came bearing the name of Donna Karan or other brands.

Unlike our regular clothing sections, the hard good sections were opportunistic. We'd sometimes get, in some stores, Laura Ashley back scratchers or loofahs. We once got some foam-covered toilet seats, which we sold out and never saw again. At holiday times we might get a few dozen leather wine carriers that retailed for $100 and we'd sell for $29.99.

But we were still at heart a men's store and following Sy's original vision, once you took the escalator down to the lower level, you were in a man's world.

This world would encompass racks with thirty feet of ties, sixty feet of five rows of men's shirts, dress, sport, and short-sleeved. Further on were floor-to-ceiling suits and sports coats, with educators and tailors waiting to help.

Because we didn't want our customers to go anywhere else, we were continually adding items we thought they'd want, including Dopp kits and the fillings for them, such as nail-clippers and travel razors. Our aim was to provide one-stop shopping.

Each department in each store kept expanding as our business grew and our buying staff grew. We'd eventually have a women's buyer (poached from Loehmann's), a men's buyer (poached from Barneys) and then give them assistants so they could maintain the relationships with suppliers while the assistants did the paperwork. All our leaders learned on the job. They all had personality and desire, which is often enough.

For me, the five years between 1978 and going public in

1983 was a time of incredible learning. I was a sponge, and Sy was my teacher and mentor.

What made us a success were the disciplines that grew up around experiencing the growth of the business early on, and how we were always more important to the vendors than the customers. That didn't mean we didn't value or respect our customers; that was our whole value system. But our importance to our suppliers—giving them cash for their overruns—made it possible to offer our customers genuine bargains. And we wanted to make it pleasant and easy for them to shop and to realize they were getting bargains. The more they bought from us, the more we could buy from our suppliers for the next season.

From that reality, we developed rules: The stores can't be near a department store. We shouldn't make it easy (pre-internet) for customers to comparison shop. We can't use manufacturer's names in advertising. Don't call markdowns a sale. All of this was to make sure the real essence of the business was preserved: the symbiotic relationship with designers that turned their overruns into cash for them. This informed Sy's decision-making every day, and it soon informed mine too.

All was not sweetness and light. I didn't challenge Sy much during the early days, but I did on some issues from time to time after a few years when I felt I had my credentials in order. Our disagreements often resulted in a better decision. Areas that seemed terribly important to me at the time included whether to keep the black interior walls in the stores or to brighten them up (I lost that one), whether to open on Sundays, and whether to offer national credit cards (I eventually won those two). Personal boundaries are important, particularly in a family business, but in any business that's high-pressure. Even though Sy and I spent many hours together visiting stores, interviewing candidates, and reviewing buys, we both acknowledged that our vacation time was personal time. That included the one day a week we were not engaged with the business.

After we expanded, we'd fly in our distant managers for meetings four times a year. (This was way pre-Zoom.) This was expensive for us, but worth the investment for the managers to hear, as a group, directly from Sy. His message was our culture, and he was the one to transmit it. The managers loved the dinners afterward where the conversations were very raucous and bonding.

Sy also liked to test out our disagreements by bringing them up at these managers' meetings. They didn't really know what to do when we clearly disagreed. I always lost in this forum—nobody would openly disagree with Sy—but he would always listen to additional evidence in later conversations.

One area of friction was Sundays. It didn't make any sense to me and the other managers that our suburban stores closed on Sunday, the busiest shopping day for suburban families. They, and I, argued to Sy that it was hurting our competitiveness, especially as we expanded into children's clothes and domestic products and became more of a family place to shop. We had the darndest time convincing Sy, and this discussion went on at every meeting—and most private conversations I had with Sy—until well after we went public.

As we expanded to Falls Church and beyond, we began to put together an operations manual. This was my job: Speak to everyone, put it all together and write parts of it, working with our eventual operations manager. I'm not sure I really appreciated it at the time, but this gave me great insight into every facet of the business.

As we grew, we naturally looked at all sorts of places to expand and different ways to do it. Through this process, which entailed many discussions both serious and not so serious, Sy was great at maintaining discipline. He didn't want to do anything outside his wheelhouse. It's important to keep in mind that all of our growth was internally financed. This gave Sy and our management team a great deal of confidence and a sense of freedom of action because we didn't have to confer with a bank on expansion decisions.

We considered licensing the Syms name in Japan, for example. This involved large numbers of Japanese gentlemen coming to our offices in Park Place, in the crumbling prewar building that didn't really have a conference room. Once about a dozen Japanese men showed up, and we met them in one of the storage rooms on the top floor, featuring rotting, exposed wood beams. At one point the leader of the group lit up a cigarette, even though smoking was frowned upon apart from Sy's pipe. Once he lit up, the rest of them all lit up too. I was running around shouting: "Ashtrays, we need ashtrays!" Sy eventually tired of the tedium of the negotiations, and it turned out we had little enthusiasm for this deal, so it never happened.

The closest we came to international expansion was in 1981 when we bought A. Sulka, the upscale men's haberdasher with stores in New York, London, Paris, and San Francisco. Sulka was almost 100 years old when we purchased it. It was the haberdashery of choice for kings, dukes, and princes. Sy liked the idea of an upscale outlet for goods that he might be able to slip into Syms stores. I loved the idea because it would be a great training ground for me with my interest in fancy fabrics. But the integration never really took off—the customer bases were just too different.

Amos Sulka started A. Sulka & Co. as a shirtmaker in New York in 1893, two decades before Morris Merinsky opened his first collars and cuffs shop. Amos moved to Fifth Avenue and opened stores in London and Paris just after World War I. Clients included the Duke of Windsor, Henry Ford, Winston Churchill, and Clark Gable. The Billy Rose character (Fanny Brice's husband, played by James Caan) in *Funny Lady*, the movie sequel to *Funny Girl*, talked about his silk

Sulka pajamas. By the 1980s, the brand had expanded from shirts to ties, silk dressing gowns, and other luxury men's goods.

Sy found out about Sulka in 1980 through his friend Irving Felt, who developed Madison Square Garden and owned the Felt Forum and also owned Sulka. Irving was operating it more as a vanity than a business, and he was getting tired of the losses. Felt wanted to dump Sulka—he just lost interest in the enterprise. Managing this type of business required acute attention to detail and oversight of aging Italian craftsmen in Como, Italy; New York, and Paris.

Sy was in love with the Sulka product and he had always wanted to add higher-priced tiers to Syms's offerings, eventually to make it more of a department store. Sulka might be one step. He knew he could get the company for a song from Irving Felt, so he pursued the deal.

I wasn't brought in on the negotiations until the very end in 1981. Sy sent me to Felt's apartment at the Sherry-Netherland on Fifth Avenue, across from Central Park, with some deal documents. He was charming, a world traveler, and not the traditional garment industry guy. He knew Sulka was a jewel, but he was no longer interested.

As soon as we closed the deal, Sy and I dove into the task of refurbishing the beautiful Sulka store at Fifty-fourth and Fifth. It was all cherrywood and mahogany and crystal chandeliers, the opposite of a Syms store. We worked on the design of the store together: We put in everything we didn't have at Syms. Fancy bathrooms. Fancy dressing rooms with doors. Upholstered chairs instead of the Syms hard wooden benches. We were like kids in a candy store. Sulka embodied luxury, not saving. We looked at Sulka as a way of experiencing retail that my dad and I had never been privileged to indulge in. We had a blast!

One issue we tried to deal with early on was the Sulka customer base. Where Syms customers were aspirational, Sulka customers had already made it. They didn't need to save a few dollars on a tie. They knew exactly what they wanted and needed to find it right then. For these guys there was no sifting through racks and racks of suits in various sizes. And they were a lot older than our staple Wall Street customers. Nearly 60 percent of them were over the age of sixty-five. They might replace worn-out items in their wardrobes, but they weren't going to expand them.

Sy flew to Paris, then I went to meet the head of Sulka Europe at the store on Rue Castiglione, a few steps from the Hotel Ritz. I was overwhelmed to see the incredibly intricate and century-old process of how things were done. The workshop was above the store and right out of Dickens. Old men in spotlessly clean aprons hunched over long workbenches using the finest of materials to hand-cut silk sleeping gowns and pajamas as had been done in that space for decades.

A Sulka smoking jacket or sleeping gown might take three months from order to delivery. My instinct was to speed it up a bit, but not too much. I jumped into trying to understand the supply chain, the production process, the marketing, and how to create more demand from customers we didn't normally cater to.

We thought a lot about silk and cashmere. I remember sending one of my father's lovely silk bathrobes to a factory in China to see if they could replicate it cheaply, that way taking a Sulka idea and making it affordable for a Syms customer. All Sulka silks were made in Italy. The Chinese company replicated it and to the letter. The robes looked identical and they even added a crumpled-up Kleenex they had found in my dad's pocket! We eventually dropped the idea.

Sulka was a different world. For me, it was like going to school for a different segment of retailing. It was also my introduction to a different kind of relationship between workers and their employers and the government. While Syms had always been a union shop, the protections for workers in Europe were far beyond anything we had. If a worker in Paris wasn't up to snuff, it was practically impossible to fire them. In London, the wrinkle was that you couldn't actually buy the property on which your store was built. Most of central London is owned by various old royal families. You might get a ninety-nine-year lease, but not ownership.

Sulka also had a store in San Francisco, which meant I got to visit one of my favorite cousins. But the store wasn't doing much business. The manager didn't seem to care about profitability. Since this wasn't Paris, we clearly needed to and could replace him.

I'd never fired anyone before. One of the reasons I enjoyed growing Syms was that I felt proud about people making a living from my dad's idea. With our name on the building, we were helping good people make a living, pay for their kids' college, and live a nice life.

Firing somebody tied me in a knot. Sy always said you have to think of the greater good. I saw that. This manager didn't respond to any of the incentives we tried or have any plans for growing the customer base. I flew out and spent a lot of time in my room at the St. Francis trying to figure out how to do this. I broke out in a rash and wasn't sleeping. I didn't talk to Sy about it because he might think I wasn't strong enough. It was one of hardest things I had ever done. Eventually, I looked him in the eyes and explained why it wasn't going to work going forward. I called it a firing, which it was. The upside is that we were able to find a replacement who brought ideas, creativity, motivation, and commitment, and he turned the store around.

The fun part of owning Sulka was the glamour, creativity, and lack of worry about markup pricing.

We expanded their lines and went into cashmere sweaters and sports coats, suede and leather jackets. We hoped this would meet the needs of growing conspicuous consumption for young Wall Streeters during the Reagan years. We did expand the market and that made it easier to sell when the time came.

Sulka had jewelry, which Syms did not. I knew nothing about cuff links or men's bracelets. We designed an insanely popular men's bracelet in the form of a long, curved-over building nail. There are takeoffs on it all over the internet, and I still have one in a box somewhere. There was also a Sulka fragrance.

We went to runway shows of all the hottest designers and picked up a lot of surplus runway dresses for Syms. But now instead of seeing them packed in boxes in New Jersey, we saw them from the front row in Paris being worn by strutting supermodels.

It was glamorous, but I tired quickly. I appreciated the creation of fashion art and the expression of how people lived in historical moments, but at heart I was still Marcy from Yonkers. Once I understood this part of the industry, it didn't have any sticking power for me. I went to two seasons of fashion shows and then stopped going.

A few years after we bought it, we saw that Sulka was taking up a lot of management time for a limited return. These sorts of judgments are vital to any business, not just a small business or a family-owned business. They are also difficult to make. Sulka was fun to own. It was something different. It was Sy's idea!

In late 1984 we decided to try to build it up to better profitability and look for a buyer.

We hired an ex-Gucci publicist who became entranced by

the challenge. We ran beautiful full-page ads in the *New York Times Magazine, Fortune, Leaders,* and other publications read by CEOs. They usually were decorated in a bubbly gold color. We produced similarly gold-hued catalogs and a fancy brochure featuring pullout pages with a picture of a Sulka product on one side and pricing information on the back, suitable for a man to slip into his inside coat jacket pocket or a woman into her purse.

We used creative merchandising ideas for attention, but also to delight those people who shopped there. It was hard to get them excited.

It worked. We managed to revive the Sulka name as a high-end luxury gift. The tie range became very profitable. We didn't have the Duke of Windsor or Clark Gable in our ads, but the ties sold themselves. Sulka ties had an extra inner lining, called a binding, which made the knot more prominent at the top. It was like making a fashion statement at the bottom of your chin. Sales took off and we managed to get a lot of product into upscale men's department store sections in Philadelphia, Chicago, and Houston.

We sold it in 1989 to the Vendôme division of Compagnie Financière Richemont, a Swiss luxury holding company that also owned Dunhill and Baume & Mercier, among other top brands. They were the perfect purchaser and, we thought, a good home for Sulka. I was saddened to learn they shut it down a decade later.

Meanwhile, at home, we made sure everyone in earshot knew Syms and our slogan.

CHAPTER 6

One-Take Marcy

I had a wet dream of Marcy Syms in a garter belt.
—Howard Stern

Three . . . two . . . one . . . action!

That's how my 1977 screen test began with my dad and Stanley, his right-hand man and window dresser, in the control room. Minutes later my father came out after I had finished reading the prompter and came very close to me and whispered in my ear, "Relax, don't be nervous. No one watches or listens that closely. Just look into the camera and imagine you are speaking to one person."

My father had asked me if I'd consider doing the ladies' commercial for Syms. At that point, he was the only one on television and he thought it was time for the ads to have a female presence, since Syms had been selling women's clothing for a few years. While I was both flattered and frightened by the whole idea, I didn't want to be a spokesperson for a company I wasn't actually a part of, and I wasn't a part of Syms at that time. But my father's suggestion started me thinking about something I could do at Syms that no one else could do.

My first commercial was at a time when women in business were dressing very conservatively. I wore a bow tie and huge, black-framed glasses with no lenses in them (I didn't wear glasses then) to make me look older and more serious. I wanted to be someone whose word you could trust. If I were playing a doctor, I would've worn a white coat. Of course, as the years went on, I wanted to look younger and ditched the glasses. Years later people asked me if that was my mother in the early commercials!

At the end of the first test, Sy said, "Yeah, you pass."

Syms's very first TV commercial, in 1974, came about because an NBC local TV salesperson told Sy that he could make a barter deal—suits for a commercial spot during a New York Giants football game. Most TV spots were thirty seconds, so a sixty-second spot was an opportunity and a challenge to fill that airtime. Sy didn't film it before the football game; he was live in the NBC New York studio. He had written a sixty-second commercial that covered all of the themes we'd later advertise over the years. And he delivered it live.

I remember our family was all together waiting for him to come on the screen. It was incredible. He had so much information to cram into sixty seconds. The experience was extraordinary. The camera was static, there were no prompts, and he literally read the equivalent of a Syms manifesto. It was all there: Name brands. Never a sale. Off-price. Fiber content. An educated consumer is our best customer. From that commercial sprang several of our first thirty-second ads.

I listened closely to how *An educated consumer is our best customer* sounded because I had suggested it should say *An informed customer is our best customer.* I thought *educated* sounded elitist. Not all of our customers might have had a college education, but anyone could be informed.

But Sy said, vociferously and correctly, that it had to be *educated* because that was aspirational. And Syms's offering of brand names at off-price was aspirational. He was right. That was a brilliant decision.

And that aspirational element to our messaging was integral to our success until we closed the stores.

Another aspirational element was sports. Sy loved to sponsor pregame shows where the host would say, "Our guest, [always a football player], is getting a suit from Syms." At the break, our ad would say that a 44 XL costs the same price as 42 regular. Years later we also created an unsung hero award, chose a player who was hard to fit, like basketball star Phil Jackson of the Knicks, and Sy would give him a suit that fit.

Sy intuitively understood that one of our unique appeals was that we would fit you and, in the 1970s, not make you pay for alterations. Bigger customers didn't have to pay extra. This remained a marketing message until the very end.

Until we closed the stores in 2011, Syms advertised on television, radio, and local newspapers in all of our markets.

We also applied the concept of off-price to how we bought radio and TV time, which partly explained how we could be on the air so often. We provided the stations with plenty of ready-to-air spots, and we had a pool of cash for last-minute buys for times they didn't sell.

We even got last-minute local spots during the Super Bowl from time to time. They had a spare thirty seconds at 49 percent of the normal run of station price, way cheaper than other local advertisers paid, and miles cheaper than the millions of dollars national Super Bowl advertisers paid. But for where our stores were, it was the same audience.

We got a similar deal once during the hugely rated CBS newsmagazine *60 Minutes* on Sunday night. There had been a plane crash and all the travel advertisers canceled, so we got a spot cheap. We were consistently in shocking places on TV. Because of these spot buys, the consumer might think we were on all the time. We actually weren't, only one week a month, but it seemed more frequent. These last-minute buys gave the impression we were punching above our weight and were a major advertiser. Our competition on TV in the New York area was Tom Carvel, the ice cream guy, and Crazy Eddie, who used an actor to manically pitch stereos and TV sets (*Our prices are INSANE!*). Neither of them appealed to the demographic we were after.

We didn't subscribe to ad measurement companies like Arbitron and Nielsen, but I became an expert in ad measurement by getting copies of the TV and radio station reports from these services and would look for the times and programs most watched by 24- to 59-year-old men and women. They were our target audience.

Despite the huge number of ads we produced, depending on the season—I remember one recommending wool blends because the price of pure wool had suddenly shot up—we spent maybe two days a year before the camera, either at a store or in a studio. We would do two or three a day. Stations would get our ads weeks before they needed to run. They loved us. No last-minute rushing and we were flexible if it didn't run because they got a higher revenue ad from someone else. We only got upset if we got bumped during a store opening.

Just as Syms didn't return unsold merchandise to the manufacturers, we never made the stations reimburse us for TV slots that didn't run or were bumped by higher paying advertisers. We'd take another ad whenever they had the time.

I recently watched them all, so you don't have to. But I imagine many of you remember them. They ran so frequently, they were hard to miss. (Some are available on YouTube and at my website.)

They worked. By the magic of repetition, they hammered home everything we needed the consumer to know. And they got people into the stores.

The message was finely tuned to stress the benefits to the consumer of shopping with us. Sy considered advertising an adjunct to his main selling proposition: Understand what your customer wants and give them that. It's no good driving people to stores if you can't make them happy to shop there.

What struck me the most after watching all of these ads was how the messages neatly tell the whole Syms story.

Here are the main messages:

- Syms has low prices.
- Syms never has a sale because we offer low prices every day.
- We have the largest selection of colors and sizes of any store in America.
- Brand and designer names mean quality. If quality suffers, the brands go out of business.
- We sell only brand and designer names. More than 200 of them.
- Our stores have no frills, so we can offer the lowest prices.
- Our labels tell you how prices go down the longer a garment is on the floor.
- The more you know about clothing, the better it is for Syms.

This was the time of Ralph Nader's consumer movement, and that spirit—that the consumer needed information—drove our commercials about fiber content, check the label for the brand, and such. They were very much a product of the time.

The commercials aren't fancy. It's usually my father or me or us both, (and occasionally one of my brothers) standing stock-still before a rack of clothing in one of our stores (sometimes taking a few steps forward) and intoning the message:

"At Syms you'll never see the word *sale*."

"Syms has the biggest selection of colors and sizes of any store in America."

"These are names you must know."

"If you know brand and designer names you'll never overpay."

"Many stores advertise fifty percent off, but if you don't know the brand, how do you know what you're buying?"

"You'll never pay more for special sizes."

"Syms—off-price, brand and designer names only.

"Our salespeople don't sell. They educate."

"If people say our stores look like warehouses, that's fine. So long as they're neat, clean, and well-organized."

"No frills means off-price. Bargains every day of the year."

"When a manufacturer makes five thousand men's suits and sells four thousand, we buy the rest. We pay less than wholesale and sell for less than retail."

"When you pay less, you can afford more."

The toughest ad to write was one about our automatic price reduction system for ladies' dresses. We needed to get so much information in 28.5 seconds and needed to make the ticket visual. I was on camera for a total of eight seconds. The rest of time it was the ticket.

From the very first commercials and in my day-to-day life, all my clothes came from Syms. We expanded the women's offering organically as more and more vendors felt comfortable with us. We even had people go to Paris and Milan and purchase discarded items from European runway fashion shows and sold one-of-a-kind couture in a separate department.

All this came gradually. One time I needed clothes for a black-tie dinner. I waited until the last minute and started looking around our Park Avenue store. There was nothing that fit me, so I confess I had to go to Bloomingdale's!

Years later, I reflected in a speech about what dressing for these ads taught me and where it led me at Syms. I also, self-servingly—because, after all, it was my job—gave some advice that I still endorse on how to compose a wardrobe.

When I first started doing the commercials in 1979, I was not only new to television pitching, but also to my role as a corporate leader. As I grew into that role and became more comfortable with who I was and what I had to say, my confidence began to show. It took a while, but I think the "TV Marcy" has finally caught up with the real-life Marcy. I don't feel at all defensive about my position. I feel, at last, like I can be ME.

Just as it took me a while to decide which Marcy I wanted to project before I could do so clearly and confidently, everyone has to decide what message they want their clothes and grooming to convey before they can expect a wardrobe to do that important public-relations job for us.

If you don't want to come home with a wardrobe that makes you look like every Tom, Dick, or Harriet—or worse, like Tom on one day, Dick on the second, and Harriet on alternate Tuesdays—you need to plan your wardrobe. It's really the best way to shop. Otherwise, you'll end up with a closet full of clothes that don't match anything. Know what you're looking for. Know what gaps you need to fill in your wardrobe. Be disciplined.

There are several good ways to get a sense of what clothes really appeal to you. One is to scout out the local department stores and to look at what is in style this year: what is being shown with what, what are the looks. Because the high-priced stores can afford to devote floor space to mannequins and fashion displays, you can walk their aisles just to get a sense of the right mixes for this year. Some years, prints are worn with prints; in other years, that look is as "out" as the polyester leisure suit. What's the ratio in width of neckties to jacket lapels? Are short skirts worn with flat shoes or high heels? Of course, you can deviate from the rules if you're comfortable with a different look, but you're best off at least starting with a working knowledge of the rules.

Sy also wore only Syms clothes. Talk about standing by your product. We knew what things really cost, so neither of us was comfortable shopping retail.

My dad always wore a neat suit and tie from the store. I wore blouses and scarves or a suit, also from the store.

Most commercials ended: "At Syms, an educated consumer is our best customer."

The thing I noticed while watching all of these commercials was that over the years my hairstyle changed from big and frizzy, to long and straight, to a bob, to a pixie cut. I purposely chose these variety of looks to make me less publicly recognizable. I didn't want to be that available to people in my private life.

My dad's hairstyle stayed the same—a small patch of hair on the top of his head. He never minded being recognized. When he walked into a restaurant, people would say, "That's Sy Syms," and he loved it.

We only deviated from the straight-to-camera approach a few times. Once was a couple of ads in 1997 when an agency persuaded us to show little cartoon labels with tiny mouths saying *I'm a Bill Blass suit. I'm a Pierre Cardin suit* and such. We dropped them after a couple of appearances. We also ran a few ads with the song "Who's Sorry Now" playing over our normal messages shown on the screen. (We only ran this a few seasons and I never really felt comfortable with this, but it was the only spot that ever won an industry award.) We also tried a few simple ads with words on the screen saying *Problem: College costs $30,000 a year. Solution: Syms: When you pay less you can afford more.*

In some of the commercials, in order to get the full impact of how long our clothing racks were, we did them in the store after closing. Sometimes our coworkers would pretend to be customers and walk by in a shot. We did them in Westchester and Secaucus, but it didn't matter because all our stores looked pretty much the same. Customers in Pittsburgh or Miami would recognize the experience of their store.

Inevitably, all that TV and radio exposure made us quasi, at least, public figures. We were certainly recognized.

Sy and I were doing comparison shopping at a giant mall in Bethesda, Maryland, outside DC called White Flint Plaza. We'd been on TV for a few years supporting our Falls Church, Virginia store. Going down an escalator, the woman behind me leaned over and asked, "Is that Sy Syms you're talking to?" I said yes. She said, "He's got such a beautiful voice." When we got to the bottom I said, "Sy, meet a customer." She said, "I was just talking to your wife."

It was that exchange that made us both realize that since I was only identified as Marcy Syms in the ads and I was trying to look older, people thought I was his wife, not his daughter. This became clearer over the years.

To this day, all those commercials seem to have stuck in peoples' minds. Not long ago I got an email that read:

Dear Ms. Syms,
I am 80 some years old and a practicing physician and when my patients tell me how good I am at explaining things, I tell them I learned this when I was babysitting my younger brother and I watched your father on channel 5 teaching us how his clothes in his store in Brooklyn were better than those from the big stores and then saying, "At Syms an educated consumer is our best customer." I've never forgotten.
Best wishes,

At a recent fundraiser on the Upper West Side of New York, Steven Spielberg's sister, Nancy, a documentary filmmaker, saw my name tag and cried: "OMG Marcy Syms! I have a great Syms story." (I love Syms stories.)

She told me that while she was living in California, she met the man she would eventually marry, who was a New Yorker. When she visited him the first time in New York, he said he wanted to introduce her to Syms, something they didn't have in California.

"I felt like a kid in a candy store," she told me. "I couldn't believe the selection and the prices." Syms became a date location. "We had so much fun and we learned so much about each other." After being a loyal Syms customer, she told me it's now hard to shop retail.

Sy wanted our holiday messages to be different from those of most other stores. We were seated in front of a Christmas tree and a menorah and a fireplace in big leather chairs. Not in a store in front of 400 suits. It was the end of the year and we weren't announcing a sale, just saying thank you for being a Syms customer. One of us always said, "We wish you a merry Christmas, a happy Chanukah, and lots of good health and prosperity in the coming year. In 1988 (or whenever) you'll never see the word *sale* at Syms. At Syms, an educated consumer is our best customer." We were making a promise— a covenant, if you will—with the customer.

My first take was always the best. Sy called me One-Take Marcy. I'd say, "Let's do another just in case," but the first one was always the best.

Radio shock jock Howard Stern started out at a local DC radio station. When we opened our store in Falls Church and advertised on his station, Howard started to do bits about me based on his having seen the TV ads.

One involved him having a wet dream about Marcy Syms doing a commercial in only a garter belt. Our coworkers didn't find this funny. I met Howard years later at an NBC event and was surprised to find that, before his make-over, he was a very shy and overweight guy from Long Island who was a lot of fun to talk to.

Another great source of free advertising was local TV. This was Sy's comfort zone since his broadcasting days. All our commercials made him well-known, and he ate it up. In the 1970s and 1980s he became something of a regular on a very popular local TV talk show hosted by Joe Franklin, another New York character if there ever was one. Joe famously sat behind a desk and because he was short, never stood up on the air. So guests like Sy had to walk over to him on the set and sit on a couch. They would talk about the old days in Brooklyn, local politics, sports, yadda-yadda, with scant, if any mention, of clothing or shopping. The two local celebrities got along great.

The TV exposure got both of us invitations to speak to Chambers of Commerce in Washington and wherever we opened a new store. This was a wonderful way to expand the brand into places that would have taken a lot longer to do if we hadn't been on TV and radio. Businessmen and women were our core market.

Sy and I were also invited to speak to many executive groups, colleges, and universities about retailing, off-price, and entrepreneurship. We'd always oblige. We happily made ourselves accessible to the local communities—great publicity for the company.

Speaking also taught me valuable lessons. The first time I was asked to speak to a college audience, because of my exposure on the TV ads, I thought it would be a good opportunity to test some ideas I had about learning and business and skills needed, but of course I also wanted to increase the awareness of Syms. I was told the presentation would be an hour, and I could expect 150 students of various college ages.

I got my notes together and thought I had a good half hour of points about habit creation and especially what you think today becomes your habits and those habits become your future. Lofty ideas, plus time for questions.

I decided that the best way to prompt myself was using 3-by-5 note cards. I had about ten cards and at least three bullet points per card and figured each note card represented three minutes, adding up to thirty minutes of presentation.

The day of the presentation, I was delighted that there were more than 150 students in the auditorium, and I was humbled by the lovely introduction I received from the business professor.

As I looked up from the podium and saw the mostly eager faces, I got a sinking feeling that perhaps this audience was looking for something a lot more down-to-earth than the stuff I had prepared. The feeling became more intense as I zipped through the note cards and literally imparted my prepared comments in just about six minutes. The only thing to do, I thought, was to tell the truth. I shared with the students exactly how I had prepared for my talk, where we were at this moment, and asked if they could help me get through it by asking me questions. I got a standing ovation at the end.

A lecture became a very interactive assembly. It taught me a very valuable lesson. Even when I was fully prepared, there was no guarantee that the preparation was going to meet the situation exactly as expected. Flexibility is not a characteristic that happens without experience. Getting to the ability to be flexible requires failures that turn into lessons and lessons that become invaluable by informing our future actions.

The ad budget was always 3 percent of gross sales. We stayed true to this for the entire life of the company. Having that discipline was helpful in making ad buying decisions, especially the year we had four store openings, and needed to squeeze all the opening promotions into that budget.

We always bought our ads across time blocks, which are on several stations within a given time period, say 8 a.m. to 9 a.m. on the dozen top radio stations in a market, to get the commuter audience. Starting with the first campaign, the idea was to buy airtime three weeks before a store opening on the local TV nightly news and morning drive-time radio. Every station would run an ad during the same window, Monday, Wednesday, and Friday. Our goal was to reach our prime audience two or three times a week. We gave our coworkers gift certificates if they vouched that they saw a commercial and noted the time and station. They were our monitors and a lot cheaper than hiring a service!

To supplement the TV and radio ads, we started a print magazine and newspaper column called *Educating Consumers*, which would usually run alongside the index page, labeled *Advertisement*. We'd give information, like a news article, about retail trends, fabric fashions that season, or things affecting prices. We also started announcing Bash in newspapers twice a year, using Roy Lichtenstein–type dot art. It looked great.

Given our communications backgrounds, my dad and I were always eager to cooperate with reporters wanting to write about us. It was great free publicity. In addition to countless local market stories when we opened, expanded or moved, we got regional or national coverage in *Manhattan, inc.* (cover headline: SY AND THE FAMILY SYMS; story headline: SAY IT AGAIN, SY) written by David Remnick long before he became editor of *The New Yorker*; *Forbes* (HI, THIS IS SY SYMS) and *Fortune* (THE MAN WHO MAKES MILLIONS ON MISTAKES), among others.

The articles were mainly favorable, but Sy didn't really

care if they weren't. He just wanted the name out there. He laughed at a *Saturday Night Live* sketch parodying our commercials with his character identified as Sly Syms.

> Both my dad and I were always very comfortable saying the words we wrote—we believed what we were saying, and we were passionate about the messages we were sharing. It was our integrity, authenticity, and honor that was on display. As someone told me after complimenting the commercials, the camera doesn't lie. The camera also picked up that Sy trusted in my integrity as I trusted in his.

Those were good times and we were soon to be a publicly traded company.

CHAPTER 7

Taking Chips Off the Table

Pressure is a privilege.
—Billie Jean King

In the winter of 1980, my father drove me home after we had both worked late at the Park Place store in New York City.

"By the way, Marcy," he said casually. "I'm going to be putting this in writing, but if something should happen to me, you'll be responsible. I hope you don't think that's too heavy a burden." I was quite simply overwhelmed.

My father's need to name a successor arose because his doctors had recently advised him of a health problem. He realized he had to start thinking about the future of Syms. At the time, four of his six children were working for Syms. The oldest male, my brother Stephen, was a buyer reporting to Sy, and my middle brother Robert was an assistant buyer. My younger brother—who viewed himself as the obvious heir apparent—was a store manager. My two sisters, the two youngest children, had not started to work yet.

Sy enjoyed leading and was good at leadership. He had an innate charisma and ability to size up a room and find the right words to get the message across. He could do that in any situation, from Joe Franklin's talk show to being honored by the Catholic Archdiocese of New York. We supported Catholic charities and virtually every other kind of good cause. Sy would say our customers are Catholics, Protestants, Muslims, Jews, Socialists, Communists, conservatives—we love them all. He was always looking to engage. This was his leadership skill.

Being the eldest of six kids, I was more detail oriented, more about management. By 1980 I was qualified and I did know the business.

Very soon after that conversation, I helped with one of Sym's biggest transformations: going public.

For any business, especially a family-owned one still being run by the founder, going public is a major inflection point. Since founding his first store in 1959, Sy had always gotten the money to open new stores through the profits he made each year. He had essentially no debt, apart from the money he owed on store leases. But by the early 1980s he had begun thinking about selling shares and gaining a New York Stock Exchange listing.

One of the first deals I was involved with Wall Street was when we got development bonds for our first distribution center in Lyndhurst, New Jersey. I did this because Sy didn't like these negotiations. He expected me and our team to deliver on his general guidelines.

In 1979 we were looking for a distribution center. Sy looked in Brooklyn and Long Island, but then he looked at the developing area in New Jersey called the Meadowlands, now one of the most developed areas in the northeast, but at that time a vacant marshland. (The Meadowlands is allegedly the final resting place of the late Teamsters president Jimmy Hoffa, who disappeared in 1975. If he's there, we never saw him. It's also the home of the stadium that hosts the Jets and Giants football teams.)

At the time New Jersey was offering development bonds to help bring business to the Meadowlands, which because of the difficulty of building on this marshland, required big incentives.

We moved into our new distribution center in 1981. For the first time, we had a distribution hub that let us much better control the cost of distribution. We could distribute some goods from this center while some stuff was still shipped directly to stores from manufacturers. It made a big difference in controlling costs, and it enabled us to better control which goods went to which stores as we grew.

This was a significant move toward being able to expand beyond the tristate area (and the small Miami and Buffalo stores) and to consolidate the executive functions like accounting and buying in one place. We were able to control costs and plan for growth. Soon after opening the distribution center in 1981, we opened a second store in Florida.

We wanted to expand in either Chicago or Boston. I did the market research on Boston while a colleague researched Chicago. Since I had gone to Boston University, I treated this as a competition I wanted to win.

I wanted to open two stores on the same day, something we had never before done. I found two good locations in the Boston area: one southwest of the city and one due north. Both were just off highway exits and in communities that satisfied our guidelines as high per capita areas.

We both made our presentations on Boston and Chicago, but I kept the fact that we could open two stores the same day for the very end.

This was a friendly intercompany business discussion, with merit on both sides. Both Chicago and Boston satisfied our criteria to consider a new market for a store. They both had more than 1.5 million people, sophisticated consumers, who had the ability to shop in many types of department stores that offered name brand and designer merchandise, and because of their size had highway systems that would allow for a destination location for a large part of the population.

My colleague Irwin went to Chicago. I went to Boston. It was fun! We would go and look and come back and report what we saw. Boston won, and I had given myself a very exciting marketing challenge.

The main challenge was getting enough goods for two 45,000-square-foot stores. On the day we opened it, I rented a car and went to see for myself. Both stores were jammed. I couldn't find a parking spot at the northern store. Going to the south, I couldn't even get off at the exit! There was bedlam. It was one of the most exciting days of my life. Boston was a very good market for us. It had lots of stores and Filene's Basement (for basement prices). People there understood us.

For the Boston openings, Sy was at one store and I was at the other. We were able to share, by phone, the incredible moment when our openings were causing traffic jams on Route 28. I will never forget this.

Chicago opened three years later, also two stores on the same day, following the Boston template.

Within three years we clearly needed a bigger corporate headquarters and distribution center, so we started looking again. (This didn't happen until 1987, when we moved a few miles from Lyndhurst to Secaucus.)

Six months before going public in 1983, we met with bankers from Rothschild and Ace Greenberg from Bear Stearns. While Sy loved to smoke his pipe and chat with Ace, I was left, happily, to do all the detail work with the actual bankers. This involved creating, for the first time, organizational charts showing who did what, who earned what, statistics on how much we sold per square foot of selling space, and dozens of other things that needed to go in the offering document, which was issued September 23, 1983, containing forty-four tightly packed pages of text and charts. I had help, but this was challenging and a lot of work. I didn't mind, because we always preached transparency—and boy, was this transparent.

All of a sudden, we were in a fishbowl. We had to become more professional and organized. The IPO process helped immensely.

Doing this work really showed me how other people would look at our organization and how the place worked. I got along great with the Wall Street folks, maybe because of my curiosity and having listened excitedly to my father talking about so many business issues since I was a little girl. It was all interesting to me, while Sy still didn't trust bankers. It didn't hurt that the Wall Street people spoke well of me to Sy.

The expectations of our growth and how many stores we could ultimately have were all tested during this process. It forced us to think these things through, not just worry about the next day's business. It was like getting a PhD in finance in six months.

Our investment bankers Rothschild and Bear Stearns were a joy to work with. They really seemed to love our business. We intentionally met with them at the stores, instead of at their lavish offices or a fancy restaurant. "Let's meet at the store!" Everyone was excited about the formula and what they were seeing in our New York City store on a Friday afternoon at 4 p.m. They invariably saw something they didn't know. "You carry Giorgio Armani! Oh, my goodness!" They always shopped when they visited. We decided to give them corporate Syms credit cards so they basically got the employee discount. This led to us establishing a Syms corporate credit card for all of our vendors. They were invariably some of our best customers.

By 1983, Syms had eleven stores: five in the New York City area (including two in the New Jersey suburbs), one each in Buffalo and Miami, two near Boston, and two near Washington, DC. The company reported $147 million in sales and profit of $7.5 million. Our margins were generally around 5 percent, healthy for a retail operation. We had more than 1000 coworkers.

Shortly after the Burlington Coat Factory went public, Sy talked with their chairman, Monroe Milstein, whom he knew and respected. Sy said after one of these meetings, "I'm going to take some chips off the table" and pay himself after two decades of effort and sacrifice. He was never materialistic, but thought he had earned this. We'd always reinvested everything in the company and disdained leverage.

He thought it was the right time, after Burlington Coat had gone public. A couple of days later Sy and I were in the car and he said, "Wall Street's nuts. They really can't get enough of the new idea in retailing."

Sy always thought financial trends were similar to fashion. They changed seemingly for no good reason and didn't make a lot of sense. The night before we went public, underwriters who were telling us they'd offer shares at $17 a share, suddenly said they couldn't guarantee this. Sy got up and said the deal was off, though he later relented. He told me: "These guys are all smoke and mirrors." Overall, he was never comfortable with bankers, although he did admire individual advisors from time to time. We never used these public funds for expansion. It was all done out of our cash flow.

The initial public offering, at $15 a share, raised $31 million while selling 20 percent of the shares to the public, mainly Wall Street firms. In a second offering in 1997 my father raised another $27 million and reduced the family share to just below 50 percent.

The IPO offering document offers a great snapshot of exactly where we were. A few excerpts:

> An important factor in the Company's growth has been its continued ability to purchase first-quality, in-season, brand-name merchandise directly from manufacturers on terms more favorable than those generally offered to department and specialty stores. Syms estimates that approximately 500 brand-name manufacturers of apparel are represented at its stores.
>
> All but one of the Company's 11 stores are located in leased facilities. In addition to the selling space noted in the following table, each store contains between approximately 2,000 to 12,000 square feet for inspection and ticketing of merchandise. During the last fiscal year, no store open throughout the year accounted for more than 14.1% or less than 5.8% of the Company's total sales.
>
> At the time, the stores were:
> New York City, New York
> Buffalo, New York
> Paramus, New Jersey
> Woodbridge, New Jersey
> Roslyn Heights, New York
> Fort Lauderdale, Florida
> Falls Church, Virginia
> Elmsford, New York
> Norwood, Massachusetts
> Peabody, Massachusetts
> Rockville, Maryland

With Sy's encouragement and the support of the under-writers, I was named president at the time of the IPO and six months later chief operating officer. I was proud to be the youngest female president of an NYSE listed company.

We went on a long road show to sell the IPO, not just on Wall Street, but also in San Francisco, Chicago, and London. We were seeking the underwriters' commitment to what they could sell, which they all did. I loved it. I took the Concorde for the first time and even got a T-shirt from the Hard Rock Cafe! Sy and I gave a slideshow to a few dozen British bankers in an old gentlemen's club. It was all very serious and grand and exhilarating; a master's class in Wall Street and the pub-lic markets and how they work.

With 3,125,000 shares now owned by nonfamily members for the first time, we were a public company.

In talking to people on Wall Street after the IPO, I knew I had to get better at discussing financial analysis, including reading balance sheets and understanding how changing one number would change many others. We established quarterly analyst calls in the first couple of years of being public.

Most of the calls had either Sy or I in attendance along with our CFO. So I took a course at the University of Penn-sylvania called "Finance for Non-Financial Managers." I rec-ommend such a course for any non-accountant. I also needed to understand boards and their responsibility to non-board members, so I took a course at Spencer Stuart, the executive search firm, on board responsibilities. I enjoyed the sense of being a perpetual student. Later, I took a real estate course at NYU. Talking to professors is really an inexpensive way to pick the brains of experts, sort of like off-price shopping, but for knowledge. Being able to constantly learn is one of the gifts of being in an entrepreneurial culture.

Looking back on the IPO with the much later experience of shutting down the company, I wrote a column for *Family Business* in 2014 that contained some harsh lessons and a warning. It was entitled "The Unintended Consequences of Taking a Company Public."

Many private business owners buy into the hype of taking their company public without fully understanding what they're getting themselves into with an IPO.

Why? Because they look at an improving economy, the projected financial rewards, and a "way out" which can be quite tempting. In many ways, IPOs may not be the best answer to raising capital. If you are finding yourself overly eager to take your company public, you might want to take your blinders off, and look at the real picture. I know, because I've been there . . . there and back.

In 2014, companies that have already priced IPOs are on the rise significantly compared to the previous year.

In 1959, my own company, Syms Corp., was founded and we took it public in 1983 when off-price retail was a hot ticket on Wall Street, much like technology companies are today. Even though I didn't take the helm until 1998, I got to see first-hand the tremendous difference between running a private company versus a public one.

In the 1980s Syms was considered a successful mid-cap public offering. It generated wealth for its shareholders and also helped to create new jobs. It also was the catalyst to help establish the Sy Syms Foundation, which has supported charitable, educational and cultural organizations for more than three decades. As is the case when any company goes public, my father and his colleagues on the board of directors ceded some control, but they did it without compromising the original Syms mission: to offer budget-savvy consumers great deals on designer clothing.

Today, Syms would be considered a micro-cap, utterly dwarfed by the mammoth corporations that dominate the business landscape. Yet, as a publicly traded company, it would be required to follow the very same regulations as its much larger counterparts, including Sarbanes-Oxley requirements (which set new and enhanced standards for financial governance). These stringent guidelines didn't exist during my father's tenure. This isn't to say executives at public companies don't or can't manage this slippery slope, but it is definitely a challenge to say the least.

Most private business owners I know understand these regulations only too well and can cite them chapter and verse. But that doesn't mean they're prepared for the crushing financial pressure that comes along with compliance—the loss of autonomy, and the scrutiny of both shareholders and Wall Street. And it hits smaller public companies that much harder.

Mary Jo White, the charismatic and forward-looking Chair of the SEC, has recognized the need to adjust regulatory expectations for different size businesses to get rid of the "one size fits all" approach to regulation. But even with her lead, any movement on the federal level will take time.

Having been down this road, I urge private firms to cherish their independence and resist the temptation. The overwhelming majority of business owners I know take tremendous pride in their organizations. They've invested more than just monetary resources in them; they've staked their reputations and, often, their senses of self and purpose in them. Ceding control via an IPO, or private equity firms and hedge funds, can quickly erode the personal relationship you have with your company—a difficult thing regardless of the short-term payoff or the potential long-term reward. Even firms that go public and stay viable for decades aren't necessarily able to keep their original missions intact or their founders at the helm. There are always unintended consequences of cashing out that can't possibly be anticipated.

If company leaders knowingly look at the IPO as an exit strategy, then it may well be a viable scenario. But for principals of small to mid-sized businesses who are personally invested in the long-term stability and viability of their enterprise, I would suggest a dose of skepticism and thinking twice before taking their company public.

Hindsight is, of course, 20/20. The fact was, we were public, and we had to try to make the most of it. It was never easy.

In our first annual report as a public company, Sy and I told shareholders that sales had risen 22 percent from the year earlier and profit was up 38 percent. We were rolling. We had spent 1983 consolidating management of the three new stores we had opened in 1982 and reported that our gross sales margins had increased by a full percentage point (to 29.4 percent, huge in retailing), while we managed our sales increase without a proportional increase in spending.

After the IPO positioned us for growth, in 1984 we opened two stores in the Chicago area on the same day, something we had learned to do in Boston. They were in Niles, to the northwest, and Addison, due west of downtown.

Apart from our small store in Miami, which served a lot of New York transplants, all our stores were on the East Coast.

Once these sites were targeted, I spent some time in Chicago learning the market and helping to negotiate the leases.

On one trip I got snowed in and was staying near the then-new Water Tower Place. I went to a movie one night in the shopping center, and standing in line I got my first real exposure to Midwest Nice. Everyone was so pleasant and friendly. After the movie I had a cup of coffee with some of my line mates, and they answered my marketing questions on how they shopped and what they looked for in a store. This was to me far more useful than a focus group.

It was clear from my going to Chicago department stores, as well as from my coffee group, that the Midwest appetite for new trends and fashions wasn't as ravenous as that of the Northeast. We would have to stock and market our stores with the understanding that, for instance, in the men's department we'd need to show more blue blazers and gray suits by Bill Blass than by Giorgio Armani, and for women, we had to make similar decisions.

During this time, manufacturers set the clock ticking for the demise of our business model two decades later. The first real outlet mall, Woodbury Common, and the biggest for a long time, opened in 1985 in upstate New York, featuring eighty different designers and manufacturers. Before Woodbury Common, manufacturers' outlets were actually attached to their factories. The new outlet malls were mainly real estate plays, and they weren't really off-price in the way we were, because the vendors specifically made merchandise for these stores. Still, they became more and more competitors to us.

This was also the beginning of the desktop computer era, at least for business. (The iPhone didn't appear until 2007). Now we were able to see fashions on the computer rather than in-person or via the fax machine. Designers eventually could manipulate those designs if retailers wanted them.

In 1987 we moved into a new, huge distribution center in

a revamped Emerson Radio factory in Secaucus, New Jersey, just down Route 3 from Lyndhurst. An older existing building, it eventually encompassed 340,000 square feet, more than three times as big as our Lyndhurst facility. Secaucus was both a distribution center and corporate office. As soon as I saw this location, I knew it was the answer. When Sy saw it several days later he broke into a big smile, which was just the reaction I was looking for.

The space enabled us to receive, ticket, stage, and turn around or hold and then locate, thousands of suits, coats, dresses, shirts, and other merchandise. In some places we could have triple hanging of suits, the highest level of which were reached with metal staircasing and catwalks. We worked with a distribution design firm out of California and an interior design firm from New Jersey. I am still friends with both of them today.

This period was also consumed with selecting and programing a proprietary computer system that could accommodate our then completely unique ticketing coordinated by color- coding sizing in each merchandise category. I and our head of distribution traveled to Ohio to the Pitney Bowes headquarters to work with their team to create a ticketing machine that could adapt to thirteen different colored tickets in six different shapes. The effort was well worthwhile. Our two companies proudly helped bring about a new generation of ticketing machines, among the first to use the computer chip.

Getting and training the additional coworkers was challenging. We hired more than a hundred people from the area and became very popular in Secaucus. I became more involved in local issues, attending town meetings on topics ranging from waste disposal to redevelopment. A whole bunch of us New Yorkers became fully involved citizens of the state of New Jersey, because this hub and our stores in New Jersey became so important to us. Even though we were known as a

New York retailer, New Jersey was where we were putting down our corporate roots.

Parts of our distribution process were labor intensive, because we used workers to affix tickets. This was not done automatically. Some merchandise, like Jockey underwear or pantyhose, went everywhere and could be drop-shipped to each store that now had our new ticketing machines, so that hand application of returned merchandise was a thing of the past. For fashion and high-ticket items, we'd need to decide what exactly to send to Chicago and what to Boston and what to New York and New Jersey, since not everything sold well everywhere. We spent a lot of time testing where to sell Chloé or Ungaro or Versace dresses and suits. The distribution center allowed us to choose what would go to each store, considering the tastes and customs and appetite for cutting-edge fashion in each place. It was a lot of detailed work, but it paid off.

Going public as we did in an enormous period of growth, we needed to adapt fast to ever-changing circumstances.

We found properties to lease wherever they met our location criteria, but these were sometimes fixer-uppers. In Pittsburgh we took over a bowling alley. It was a 45,000-square-foot building that would eventually make a great store. But we found every imaginable problem: asbestos, underground fuel tanks, bowling shoes in the oddest places. We encountered a lot of cost surprises in this conversion. Opening dates, merchandise deliveries, coworker schedules all got fouled up. (Tactics can change, but not core identity that is consumer facing, and consumers were changing.)

My next challenge was trying to get more women into the store to shop for themselves, especially during the day. It took some doing.

Going public put me in the spotlight in a way that even doing local TV commercials hadn't done. There were very few female COOs or CEOs. As a female at a family business,

I realized early the importance of outside organizations to give me perspective and support. In 1983 I looked around for programs I could join as a female president of a public company. A Yonkers neighbor who played cards with my dad years earlier had told me about the Young Presidents' Organization.

The YPO was founded in 1959 by then twenty-seven-year-old Ray Hickok in Rochester, New York. It's a great place for under-forty-five-year-old C-suite executives to meet, exchange ideas, and for the younger generation of family business leaders to support each other. What I didn't realize when I joined in 1983 was that I would be the first and only woman in the New Jersey chapter. I eventually moved to the New York chapter, where there were a few more of us.

Still, it was mainly guys. Being a daughter and having three brothers, I got tired of always having to explain the woman's point of view. I wasn't sure how helpful I was being and the YPO didn't really fulfill my need for a gang.

I never really found the perfect organization for my specific case, so I helped start one. I had become friends with a pioneering expert on the women's role in family business, Dr. Fredda Herz Brown. We, along with one of her colleagues, started a group called Daughters of Bosses. It lasted a few years, but it turned out that most of the women drawn to membership were not only in their prime career-building years, but also in their family-building years, and their time was not their own.

Being a woman in my position at this time made my experience unique. I had heard about the recently formed Committee of 200, a group of female entrepreneurs and business leaders that started in Los Angeles, and I managed to get myself invited to join. This made a huge difference. From the first meeting I attended, I heard other women talking about making deals, hiring people, firing people, getting a loan from a bank, hiring a law firm, changing course with consultants. I realized I wasn't alone after all.

In 1988 I also joined the New York Women's Forum, comprised of women from a variety of backgrounds, united by visibility and prominence in their lives and careers. This was very helpful. No one should go it alone.

A lot of situations I was put were challenging. At a National Association of Female Executives conference on entrepreneurship in 1995, every speaker got a strict twenty-minute time slot. Once the speaker ahead of me got started, we all knew there was no way she'd finish in anywhere near twenty minutes. The control room went bonkers as she neared the thirty-minute mark with no end in sight. The producer told me I had to cut half my speech. I told him I couldn't do that, but instead I would explain to the audience that because of the WONDERFUL presentation we had, I was going to try to bullet-point mine as much as possible. I managed to make my points in a way that left the audience relieved after the previous long-winded presentation. There are often moments when we have to protect ourselves in difficult situations with dignity, integrity, transparency, and honesty.

It became clear that I needed to understand and nurture relationships with other managers in the company. It wasn't easy, at least at first. Even though I was a member of the family that owned and ran the business, I heard that behind my back I was called a bitch, that somebody said they could see my nipples through my blouse (so I started wearing Band-Aids under my shirt), and a variety of other derogatory comments. I quickly learned I wasn't the only female leader enduring this stuff, but I found that being aware of it helped me navigate around surprises.

Sometimes the disrespect wasn't overt. Lots of times coworkers who didn't like one of my decisions tried to get around me and go straight to Sy. Even though it usually didn't work, given how much we talked, it sometimes did. This went on for a good many years. But over time Sy came to see how playing one against the other undermined the whole management team, and he put a stop to it.

I decided to convene more management meetings. I had an open-door policy—anyone could drop in. I also subscribed to the idea of management by walking around and felt completely comfortable knocking on a door and popping in for a casual conversation.

Overall, I found the whole experience energizing. I liked waking up in the morning and looking forward to each day. If I were a son, I don't know that I would have had as many invitations for public-facing events. Female COOs and CEOs were still kind of unique. I remember noticing Jill Barad, the first female CEO of Mattel, the maker of Barbie, on the cover of *Fortune* magazine in 1997, and thinking you had a window of two years after you were on the cover of *Fortune* to make it or not. (Jill lasted three years.)

You were a magnet that attracted relentless curiosity, investigation, and reporting of your every move. In many cases it was almost like people saying: "You can't have this. You don't deserve this. Why you?" I recall a study of hedge funds involved in hostile takeovers being literally more hostile when the target had a female CEO. I lived through it.

Even today, the gender gap persists. While there are a handful of high-profile female CEOs, a recent newsletter from *Fortune* magazine pointed out the average tenure of a female *Fortune* 500 CEO was 4.5 years, compared to 7.2 years for men. That's just a bit better than it was in 2014, when women averaged three years to eight for men.

Familiar problems remain. Many companies don't do enough to help executives manage families as well as their jobs. There isn't a deep bench of female middle-management ranks yet at many companies, although this is gradually changing as more female MBAs and lawyers are minted.

For me, despite the resentment I felt from some coworkers

at first, I always felt comfortable in my role, and was able to grow. In the beginning, Sy did the merchandising, since he knew all the vendors, and I did the operations, an area in which he was less interested. The final decisions always rested with Sy, as they should. I was fine with that.

As I learned, I enjoyed being able to be the one to set the standard of performance and behavior. I saw it as an enormous opportunity, responsibility, and privilege to be a female looked at in this way. I embraced it. My dad saw it and it filled him with a lot of joy.

When we opened Boston in 1982, I got myself a mink jacket as a reward. I worked with the noted furrier Fred Gelb to design it. I walked into the office wearing it one day, and Sy asked where I got it and who made it. "It looks good," he said.

"Hey, Dad, did we ever consider carrying furs?" I asked.

That was the germ of an idea that grew into Marcy's Place, a name Sy chose for a separate room in twenty of our stores, usually at the back of the women's department. It had its own fitting area with a curtain.

It featured not just furs, but also haute couture dresses from Paris, Italy, and runway accessories that we received in boxes after Fashion Week: expensive handbags and other surprises. (I remember getting a towel one time.)

In addition to furs from many brand names including Bill Blass, Albert Nipon, and Mary McFadden, Marcy's Place was really a couture dress section; maybe a stretch for Syms, but congruent with our owning Sulka at that time.

Selling couture is like selling oil paintings. Selling designer dresses is like selling signed lithographs. Selling mass-produced name-brand dresses is like selling posters. They're all art and they all have unique price points, loyalty, and brand expectations that our consumer brought to each purchase.

We were great at selling lithographs and posters, and now we had some oil paintings. The couture dresses went for much higher price points, often the highest in the store except for the furs. We could offer a $2,000 dress for $599.

The higher price points, especially for furs, led us to adopt the plastic security tags that were starting to be seen in all department stores. We had always resisted them as alien to our customer-first culture.

Given the higher prices, we had a separate register and security inside Marcy's Place. You would leave with a bag or box closed with a staple gun. The door security could see the stapled receipt and if the bag was open would ask to look inside.

One of the more entertaining experiences around establishing Marcy's Place was the added security, which included a demonstration from a security company on how fur coats are stolen. What we saw was a rubber mat put on a woman's upper thigh, below her skirt. She then rolled the fur coat up to the size of a toaster oven and placed it on the rubber mat stretched between her legs and smoothed down her skirt. It was amazing!

The security tags back then were primitive. If you were a professional shoplifter, you could undo them with a small screwdriver. They didn't yet have the colored dye they have now.

We rolled Marcy's Place out to markets that had the highest per capita income concentrations, including Miami, Washington, Atlanta, Dallas, and Houston. I loved that we were able to make this work.

Around the same time, we also started selling women's hats. I wore hats all the time in the 1980s. I made sure we had a fabulous hat department, emphasizing big, colorful church hats. At Easter you wanted to go Syms for our great selection of the best-priced hats for the Easter parade.

We were now becoming a one-stop shopping experience for off-price apparel, accessories, and some home goods. Our customers continued to expect us to offer the best brands. We had established their trust over the years and it paid off mightily in the 1990s. Even as vertical retailers like The Limited, Ann Taylor, Zara, Men's Wearhouse, and Today's Man proliferated, we kept our niche and remained consistent to our core promise.

We carefully changed tactics, but still catered to the core expectations of our customers. It got messy.

CHAPTER 8

Stick to Your Knitting

Failure is success in progress.
—Albert Einstein

The 1990s, in management theory terms, was a decade bracketed by two bestsellers: *Leadership Secrets of Attila the Hun* by Wess Roberts in 1990 and *Good to Great* by Jim Collins in 2001.

The books reflected a shift in thinking from the top-down management style, in which managers ran every detail, to a bottom-up style that valued input from the people on the front lines.

The new bottom-up style appealed to me more than the older top-down approach.

Things were visibly changing for women in middle management and in entrepreneurship. Statistics showed that women, who in 1990 were already over half of the workforce, were leaving corporate jobs to start their own companies and set new rules. Technology made it possible for executives to do ever more work, to seem bigger than you were. With modest computer skills you could prepare presentations that just a decade earlier might have required three staff members to accomplish. Many women took this opportunity and ran with it.

Meanwhile, our world was changing permanently as barriers to entry in the industry kept falling. Brands like Bill Blass, Ralph Lauren, Calvin Klein, Tommy Hilfiger, and Liz Claiborne were being monetized, including the brands themselves, creating full product lines associated with their brands. These expanded lines often showed up as branded sections in department stores, a new way to merchandise and control brand dilution.

Our buyers were always going to department stores to see what was selling and what was hot. They began seeing more branded second-tier merchandise made especially for these department store sections, offering goods that could be sold for lower prices than normally associated with that brand. If you could buy a Ralph Lauren belt for $20, it was still a Ralph Lauren belt, and it undercut our pricing on similar goods.

Sy often said we needed to "stick to our knitting" in the face of business challenges and keep doing what we did best.

Our 1991 annual report offered shareholders a reaffirmation of what we were always about, along with some insights into the changing market. We explained our five principles of off-price retailing.

- Buy brand names at, or close to, manufacturer prices. Both ends of this sentence are equally important. We will not buy any brand unless we can profitably sell it at 40% to 70% regular retail. We will not buy non-branded merchandise regardless of how low we can sell it. Our credibility is at stake every day. We promise the consumer brand names. We promise the consumer 49% to 70% less than regular stores. This is what we must deliver. Every day.
- At Syms our guideline is that a deal is good only if it is good for both sides. In return for selling to us at cost, our sources know that we will pay when we

promise and make no advertising claims or demand mark-down allowances. We will never advertise their brand at low prices. These are promises we have never broken in 32 years.

- We sell to consumers at 40% to 70% below normal retail. Even though we buy for less than discounters, our markups generally do not exceed theirs. To do this we must operate a "no-frills" company. At Syms the customer won't find frills such as fancy fixtures, personal dressing rooms or gift wrapping. We cannot accept national credit cards. By not providing these extras, we give the consumer a clear choice—frills or lower prices.

- When we say selection at Syms we mean hundreds of brand names. Sizes that go up to 54 in men's regular, long, extra-long and portly. The queen's sizes in women's wear up to size 46, dresses in half sizes to 24.5. Enough colors and styles so that a customer can choose from 100 or more bargains. We make deliveries of fresh merchandise to our stores at least once a week and keep our inventories attractive with new seasonal merchandise.

- Syms operates large stores, from 25,000 square feet to 90,000 square feet. We must make shopping easy in such large spaces. We group dresses, sportswear, men's suits, shirts, etc. without regard to manufacturer. We make it easy to find a size by color-coding price tags. We carefully train our educators so they can explain how to successfully shop Syms.

We also recognized the very real challenges to this philosophy, which we'd see play out for the next two decades. We recognized that discounters were adopting many of our practices, including no-frills warehouse stores, and slashing amenities and markups. But we were confident that they would still need to pay wholesale for their merchandise, while we would pay less. That would prove true for a while, anyway.

We continued to try to represent full-quality, in season, name brands at off-price. This was still different from what big competitors like T. J. Maxx or Marshalls or Loehmann's did. They stocked their shelves with an enormous array of planned manufactured products.

All of a sudden, it seemed to me, manufacturers found a way to expand and protect their brands that didn't necessarily include Syms. This affected us and our consumers' experience of name brands.

At the start of the 1990s, we were the third biggest retailer selling tailored men's clothing (not counting department stores). It wouldn't last.

With new brands producing vast quantities of lower-priced goods because of those lower barriers to entry, we no longer had a clear field. Along came Men's Wearhouse and Today's Man, among others. They were doing the same thing we did, often with the same manufacturers. As the decade progressed, it became more of a challenge to get that first appointment or first phone call to get the first crack at that season's goods.

Sy's notion—that if we went out of business the customer could shop elsewhere, but manufacturers would have no buyers for their excess goods—was coming apart.

Men's Wearhouse was founded in 1973 in Houston by George Zimmer, after he had worked a few years for his father's apparel business. (Sound familiar?) He rapidly built up a chain and began TV advertising in 1983, appearing in the ads himself and closing with the slogan: "You're going to like the way you look. I guarantee it." (Sound familiar?)

Men's Wearhouse grew into a behemoth, eventually encompassing more than 1200 stores under several brand names. The stores were generally smaller than ours, but often in the same areas. We sometimes joked that we did their market research for them, because it seemed that wherever we were, they cropped up. Ironically, in 2009 we were the last two interested parties for the purchase of Filene's Basement. Unfortunately, Syms won.

We didn't have much personal interaction with Mr. Zimmer. Mr. Zimmer's board messily fired him in 2013.

Today's Man was another competitor, mainly on the East Coast. It was founded in 1971 in Philadelphia by David Feld, who had worked in his parents' apparel store. (Sound familiar?) They offered both designer and private label suits and other men's accessories, and eventually expanded to twenty-five stores, mainly in the Philadelphia, New York, and Washington areas. They went public in 1992, but soon thereafter faced several business setbacks and filed for bankruptcy in 1996. Mr. Feld was "temporarily" laid off in 2003. The company went out of business that year.

After we went public in 1983 for $15 a share, our stock price never really did much. Maybe analysts and fund managers didn't see us as a long-term buy. This always rankled Sy, and he said in several interviews that he "was bad at Wall Street."

In 1995, with our stock price in mid–single digits, and threats from the exchange that we might have to delist if we didn't meet certain measures, we investigated—with the help of an investment banker—the option of going private.

The idea for our possible delisting from the NYSE came from our corporate counsel, who had been dealing with the rising costs of being a public company and the shrinking of our shareholder base to fewer and fewer holders. We were running close to or below the required number of shareholders. Both Sy and I felt that if there was a way to keep our shareholders but not have the expense of being on an exchange, we should do that. During a board meeting, we asked our corporate counsel for options. After research, they came back with alternatives.

One was to make an announcement that for so many quarters we were not fulfilling the requirements for the number of holders, and we were going to delist in an orderly process. We estimated about a million dollars a year in savings by not being on the exchange.

Because of Sy's and my enthusiasm, we convinced the board to go ahead with the plan. After consulting with lawyers and bankers, we announced on August 30 that we would buy all of the 20 percent of the stock we didn't own for $8.75 a share, essentially taking the company private. It would cost about $31 million.

This deal divided the family. My two brothers, who were working at the company at the time, said it would be the "deal of the century" because we would no longer have the pressure of addressing some of the issues that could require some reengineering of our brand. We could be a lot more agile as a private company than as a public company, where every quarter everything had to be explained. I agreed wholeheartedly and gratefully took up the assignment.

We had to keep it all quiet, to prevent leaks of insider information. Acting in secrecy was a strain.

At no time during the course of this investigation was it ever considered that we'd be taking the value of the real estate that we'd acquired out of the company or separating it into a real estate investment trust, as was being done by some retailers and was suggested by an activist shareholder. Clearly, real estate appraisals are easy to have done on owned properties, and that would have been part of the valuation. If we spun those off, we'd pay a lower price to buy back the shares, at the expense of our shareholders. We didn't really know the exact price we'd have to pay the shareholders, but my brothers and I felt confident we'd be in a position to pay off the revolving debt we'd use to buy the shares.

This was confidence Sy didn't have. He worried that if we somehow couldn't pay off the debt, lenders would seize our assets.

"I don't want them to own my inventory if anything happened so we couldn't repay the debt," was his thinking. Still, we went along with the preparations.

We were ready to go by October. Everything was set with Bank of America. Projections showed we could pay off the debt we'd use to buy the stock in five years. The papers were ready to sign.

Sy called me at 7 a.m. before a 9 a.m. meeting and said we couldn't sign. "I had a dream," he told me. "I dreamed we couldn't pay off the debt and we lost everything." I told him that couldn't happen, but he wouldn't budge. We called it off.

My job was to tell all the lawyers and bankers we were canceling the plan. They looked at me like I had two heads.

This was an unmitigated disaster. In point of fact, it put us on the dashboard of every aggressive hedge fund on Wall Street. The lesson from this very painful period was to separate your insight and experience from the cheerleading and follow the analysis of the market. No matter how logically you see something, the market may see it differently.

Not surprisingly, our stock, which had been trading at $9 a share, fell to $7.50 the next day. Our continuing good results sent the shares up above $15 for a while during the late 1990s, but it slipped below $5 by 2000.

In addition to this abortive going private attempt, around 1990 and later around 1996 Warren Buffett expressed interest in Syms.

Mr. Buffett, often called the world's most successful investor, always did his homework. He only invested in companies he really believed in and understood, and generally left management in place. I was intrigued.

I responded to Mr. Buffett's letter to Sy by putting in a call to Mr. Buffett's longtime secretary. I was impressed that the phone was picked up after the third ring, and upon hearing my name, she said, "Oh, hello," as if out of the hundreds of calls she made for Mr. Buffett, she was waiting for me. It immediately felt inviting.

She put him on the phone, and Warren Buffett quickly demonstrated his ability to put anyone he engaged with on an equal playing field with himself. I was nervous; he was friendly and charming. We agreed to meet for lunch when he was next in New York at the Park Lane, his favorite hotel. Before the meeting, I tried to research everything I could in the public domain on Warren Buffett, his enormous career, and his astounding success as an investor. Everything I learned about him contributed to my feeling of good fortune to be able to sit and hear why he thought Syms would make a good investment.

What we ordered before diving into the business conversation was a bit of a surprise. Mr. Buffett had a cheeseburger with a glass of milk and French fries. I had my usual Cobb salad with the dressing on the side, hold the peppers and the bacon.

The time went quickly. I regret not immediately writing down the exchange. He did say he compared the Syms story to the See's Candies story, in that he found it a successful formula to invest in a founding family that had created a special niche within their market and had disciplined execution. He had bought See's in 1972 and still owns it.

We didn't talk dollars or cents or timing, but both Sy and I were impressed that only a couple of weeks after our first meeting, his office reached out. At this point, Sy organized a family meeting.

Sy always said he didn't want to answer to anybody, but I pointed out that being public meant we had a lot of bosses (the public). Sy had pretty much shrugged off the first Buffett approach, but in the half-dozen years since then the market had changed and I thought we could use the help.

Sy called everyone in the family together and took a poll, which was stated in a way that clearly showed his dislike of the offer. He mentioned that he thought we had a great expansion plan and "we can do this ourselves." The motion failed.

Without the Buffett investment, or going private, and with the new competition, we needed to create a new covenant with our consumers. One thing that differentiated us from our competitors was our huge selection. You could always find your size in whatever color you wanted, and you wouldn't pay extra for large sizes, as was the case elsewhere. We also kept the automatic markdown system, which nobody else had. We ran a lot of TV ads touting these two things, even though they were both loss leaders for us. But they maintained our promise to consumers.

My team was happy to handle most of the expansion work. During the 1990s we went from twenty-five stores in 1990 to forty-six in 2000. I was constantly on a plane, scouting locations, dealing with leases, supervising hiring, setting up ad campaigns, and making sure supply chains worked.

We generally spaced out openings with two or three months in between. You wanted to inventory up before Easter (winter to spring) and August (back to school and fall), so we geared our openings to the calendar. We planned our inventory purchases and what we planned to show, and left enough budget open for last-minute purchases that would be available immediately before store openings.

Usually this meant personal visits to manufacturers' showrooms and buying up their floor samples. Once Sy went up to Ralph Lauren to see the brand's new children's line. We had been supportive of the children's venture since Ralph started the division, and it fit perfectly with our expanding our children's offerings. We had a great relationship. When Sy mentioned we had three store openings coming up within six months, they were willing to sell all of their uncommitted hanging merchandise to us.

These sort of deals happened often because of our long-standing relationships of trust and respect. They knew they'd never get anything back. Whatever the problem, we'd find a price we could sell it for.

We planned for stores in the pipeline, with the knowledge that it took at least six months to retrofit a building we might want to lease or acquire.

In order to open twenty-one stores in ten years, we needed to look at some properties that weren't quite traditional for us. The old rule that they needed to be at the intersection of two big roads and be freestanding sometimes bent to reality. We wound up in a few strip malls that had housed a supermarket we could repurpose. It might not have been in keeping with our DNA, but under time pressure we wanted to do it. This necessitated entering markets that were smaller in population and per capita income, than we did during our first thirty years in business.

For the first time we opened stores in Tampa, Charlotte, Pittsburgh, Cleveland, and Rochester, New York. These were all great places, but smaller cities than we'd been used to. This required us to have different sales expectations. Here expectations were for lower volume, so we needed realistic budgets for the cost of the property, the cost of retrofitting, and our budgeting for the flow of merchandise was different. A New York area store might do $30 million a year, while Charlotte did $3 million a year.

The effort needed to open a store, whether in Charlotte or New York, was pretty much the same. You needed the same logistics, communications, operations and buying staff. It was all an adjustment and learning process. Our culture of strong communication among store management and corporate, buyers, and educators helped us make these adjustments in real time.

There were also regional differences in shopping habits. Peak shopping hours were a bit different because the suburbs and rural areas near them didn't work on the same nine-to-five, Monday through Friday clocks. There were also much relaxed dress codes for men and women.

We also had to adjust to this change. While many men were uncomfortable in department stores, our male shoppers really liked to shop. They enjoyed it because of our organization and efficiency. They could find their size, color, and brand, and walk out with a suit in a few minutes, perhaps with a joke to the educator and cashier on the side.

Instead of buying three suits a year, as our urban customers did, they maybe bought one suit every two years. Over the course of 1980s, 1990s and 2000s, men's departments in department stores became less real estate for suits and more room for everything else. Men's separates never took up as much space for us as suits. Children's, housewares, and gifts didn't bring in the same margins. We needed to sell three-sheet sets by Vera Wang to make up for one sports coat.

We needed to balance and address the changes in the male shopper. We grappled with this, but there was no quick fix. How would we make up those sales?

CHAPTER 9
Decisions, Decisions

No *is a complete sentence.*
—Anonymous

Emotionally, the disappointment of not being able to fulfill the plans to take the company private in 1996 extended well into the next year.

My brothers and I had been totally in favor of taking the company private. We didn't see a way we could thrive in the changing environment. We clearly had to do something different. Just look around. There were chandeliers in the bathrooms at Saks OFF 5th. Men's Wearhouse was everywhere. Sy wasn't the only clothing pitchman all over the TV. Manufacturers had many more outlets—including their own outlet stores—for any excess merchandise.

It became harder to understand the value proposition of being a Syms customer. It was ten years before the end, but the signs were already there.

It was much harder for us to make needed changes in a public setting, not the least of which was hiring professional managers outside the family to challenge our assumptions and test out new ideas.

Maybe in my enthusiasm I might not have listened to Sy

closely enough to see he wasn't interested. It all boiled up again in 1997.

As I wrote in my book *Mind Your Own Business and Keep It in the Family* (MasterMedia, 1992), working for and with my father, as in any family company, was a delicate balance of creative compromise and effective communication. A perfect example was a conversation I had with my father in our office, in March 1997, which probably never would have happened if the going private deal had succeeded.

I was so affected by it that I wrote it down verbatim.

As background, let me explain that since I signed on in 1978, I had worked nineteen years, never taking as many as ten days off a year. I was tired. Physically and emotionally tired. Family business was a twenty-four-hour, seven-day-a-week proposition. I had soldiered through a recession, several family breakups, exponential growth, traveling sometimes two weeks a month, and my own health issues. And I was still ticked off about the going private fiasco and the rebuffs of Warren Buffett.

It started with a seemingly trivial, but somewhat typical question from Sy as to why I had moved the men's shoe department in our Atlanta store from the first floor to the second floor, next to children's shoes. (He had just visited there; we had actually moved the shoe department two years earlier.)

"It looks funny there," he said.

"The guys (coworkers) said the men's department was too cramped and they needed the space," I replied.

"But you'll cut into sales because it's now too small."

"Well, you can look into it," I said and walked out, noting in the diary that I was showing frustration. But as I remember, I thought it best at that point to drop the mic and leave the room.

Sy had sensed this too and came back later to ask why I seemed defensive. That's when the dam burst. I told him I was tired of being second-guessed for the past nineteen years and felt I couldn't get a lot of my ideas heard or implemented. These ranged from where the men's shoe department was in Atlanta to the placement and size of our signage, to suggesting we try something other than black walls in our interiors, to a chain of small men's stores I wanted to open. This would have been a chain of Bill Blass factory outlets. We never did them.

I felt it was time Sy relinquished some of the day-to-day decision-making and become more of an executive board chair. By 1997 we were being besieged on all sides by competitors like Mervyns, Nordstrom Rack, Saks OFF 5th, and outlet stores being established by our suppliers to sell their own wares. I felt deeply that we needed to try new things, or we'd be overwhelmed by competition.

He replied, "Well, if you divert your energies, you lose something—you could hurt the business."

I changed the subject and said I wanted to take the summer off, sort of a sabbatical after nineteen years.

"But doesn't the new plan for growth excite you?"

"Frankly, no. I wrote that plan in 1986!"

"So now you can do it."

"That's just it. I'm your daughter. I have your ambition, if maybe not your courage, and I thought I'd be running things by now."

"So you feel like you're waiting for me to die?"

"If I felt that way I'd have to leave. No, I was waiting for you to retire, but I know now you won't."

"I was thinking of making you CEO and me chairman."

"That's only a title. It doesn't really change much."

"I could come in three days a week."

For several days following this exchange, we had discussions about the future of the business and our roles within it. Bottom line: Sy wasn't going to cut back any time soon, and he did not want to alter our business model. He felt that such a move was fraught with unnecessary risk.

During this period, I saw the value in pursuing therapy for myself. By that point I felt that if I was going to be able to create some personal boundaries with my siblings and parents that could work for me within the family business, I would need outside professional help in doing it in a way that was sensitive, productive, and fulfilling. After researching several people, I was fortunate to be introduced by a friend to Dr. May Markewich. She was perfect for me—already well beyond mid-career, married to a judge, with two grown sons, and an early graduate of Cornell.

I looked on her as a role model for her solo career as a practitioner and a lifelong learner, interested in business and human organizations.

After eight years she said, "You don't need to come anymore." I said, "Yes I do!" I went less frequently for another two years. We kept seeing each other for coffee twice a year until she died.

After she died, her son gave me a copy of a poem, author unknown to him or me, in her handwriting. I have it framed and on my office wall. The poem begins:

Let two men stand on a grassy sward,
That night's chill dewfall yet is pearling.
And one will glimpse a foreign field
And one behold a sheet of sterling!

It goes on to describe the difference between people who meet adversity and those who crumble.

All the years of understanding my emotions and realizing I didn't always have to act on them immediately, that I could take time to manage and describe my emotions, really came to the fore during this conversation.

But for Sy, it only seemed to strengthen his conviction that he needed to take more chips off the table, not for himself, but rather for the Syms Foundation. He thought that with a larger foundation there would be more opportunity for him to spend more time on philanthropy.

Sy did take some more chips off the table with a secondary public stock offering in the fall of 1997. This netted around $27 million, but the family lost majority control. He did use the funds for the foundation, which exists to this day.

Late in 1997, once the secondary offering was completed, he began talking to me about my becoming CEO. The board voted me in as CEO in January 1998. Sy began taking more time off, but there still was never a sense that my being CEO and his being chairman meant I didn't need to confer with him about most decisions.

For example, we always had paper bags in the store. I embraced recycling early on. The shopping bags and boxes were black paper or cardboard with *SYMS* in silver.

At one point after I became CEO, we received a big, defective order and all the bags were breaking. I thought it would be a good time to redesign them, maybe with a slogan rather than just our names. We decided on *I'm an Educated Consumer*. This was a good idea and it could have been approved in one conversation. Instead, it took several months before we got the whole team excited about the change.

The broader issue after the 1997 secondary offering was that we were no longer a family business. We didn't have majority control. Sadly, my brother died in August 1998, and my youngest sister died in June 1999 of the same heart condition. Meanwhile, my youngest brother was suing my father in part because he thought he was the heir apparent and should be treated as such. That case dragged on for five years before it was dismissed. Unfortunately, it left irreparable wounds.

The rest of the decade was consumed with hysteria about

whether all the world's computers would go haywire on January 1, 2000, the dot-com bubble bursting, and the soon-to-begin recession. Though it seems a little silly now (nothing happened), Y2K did focus Syms, and everyone else, on updating our technology (which might have been why nothing happened).

We went from fax machines the size of toaster ovens in every store to a system-wide control room in Secaucus with eleven technicians. Technology was our competitive edge, allowing us to communicate seamlessly with all our stores on inventory, sales data, and everything else. It really was a competitive advantage, but the industry was moving fast and to keep ahead required constant updating, reeducation, and continuing costly investments.

I took the lead on all the technology stuff. Sy never really got comfortable with it.

Technology continued to march on. Manufacturing improvements in programming, machinery, and robotics meant that irregulars, once 7 percent of total production and Sy's original breadbasket, shrunk to less than half of 1 percent. We had adapted over time to not being able to have this classification of product.

During the 1990s the demand for children's clothing grew rapidly, along with the millennial uptick in births. Our Syms kids departments were in most of our stores and also grew rapidly. We tested Syms kids for toddlers, and even designed a play area with toys for them to enjoy while their parents shopped. We amplified the experience by providing information for parents in the store on how to equate their children's height and weight to the appropriate size, up to sizes 12 and 14. We also created videos with a TV in the areas to constantly run things like *Sesame Street*.

Our children's section developed its own customer base. For our older customers, it was for their grandchildren, and for our prime customers, it was their growing families. We were beginning to have a reputation as a dependable off-price retailer for all things kids.

But Sy never got behind it. His history and contacts were still very firmly in the world of men's clothing, and men's clothing continued to be the largest department in every Syms store, both in real estate and in price points.

Reorder times also shrank with computers tracking every sale in real time. The formula that had worked so well for Syms in our first three decades needed to be reformulated. We still needed customers to feel we were unique in some way (like staying open late on Saturday for Hasidic communities in New York and New Jersey). One other example was waiters.

We were long known as the place that waiters in tablecloth-and-above restaurants went for their black suits. They could always find a suit in their size for $199. In the face of heightened competition, we actually lowered that to $119, which we could do because manufacturers passed on lower costs to us.

At Syms, we never price gouged. Greed was never part of the equation. Sy's goal was that our first markup be 40 percent. We didn't often make that, but we didn't aim to go higher.

While we were sticking to our knitting, the world changed in one day. Right in our backyard.

CHAPTER 10

The Day the World Changed

In preparing for battle I have always found that plans are
useless, but planning is indispensable.
—Dwight D. Eisenhower

On September 11, 2001, I was on my way to our store on
Trinity Place, a five-story former Manufacturers Hanover bank, all cinder block and cement, no windows, a perfect city store a block south and a block east of the World Trade Center.

I was stuck in the car around 8:50, which I later learned was just after the first plane struck the North Tower. All traffic was stopped on Ninth Avenue going south. I turned on the news on the radio. Oh my God. Oh my God. I eventually got back to our Fifty-seventh Street apartment. When I saw my four-year-old I burst out in tears, I was so happy to see him. Even then, it was obvious to me that nothing would ever be the same in my lifetime.

Miraculously, the only damage to the store was the shattered glass on the fifth-floor skylight. The whole area was closed. We were the first in the area to reopen just four weeks after the attack. We were able to do so because of the limited damage we had. Once the subway was running, we were back in business. Much of our customer base there in lower Manhattan commuted to work from Brooklyn, Queens, and Staten Island. They eventually returned to their offices.

> It was hard to be down at the site and not feel tears involuntarily well up and spill down your cheeks. Two of our coworkers at the Trinity Place store, a tailor and an assistant haberdashery manager, had spouses who perished that day in the Towers. I, of course, thought a great deal about being an employee of the first tenant in 1 WTC in 1974, Special State Prosecutor Maurice Nadjari, on the fifty-seventh floor.
>
> By the time I left Nadjari's office to attend graduate school at Boston University, the ground-level stores were almost all full and the Windows on the World restaurant had opened. I had met my father for lunch once there on a slow, hazy summer afternoon. Now it was all gone.

I found the government response at times absurd. President George W. Bush likely meant well when he said consumers should go out and shop to show Al Qaeda they couldn't change our way of life, but I thought that was offensive, condensing democracy down to shopping. As we discussed at the office, the country needed to focus on what was important about our system and strengthen that.

9/11 changed habits. Fear and uncertainty led to a recession that we felt deeply. Sy and I posed together for a full-page newspaper ad that said in blaring black type: **WHILE THE COST OF LIVING CONTINUES TO GO UP, PRICES AT SYMS CONTINUE TO COME DOWN.**

After the dot-com bubble and the Y2K hysteria, consumers were demanding changes in the workplace. One of them was the increasing popularity of casual Fridays, something we'd been discussing at merchandise meetings with Sy for some time. Our idea was to offer suit separates. This meant that men, who would normally just pull matching suit pants and jacket from a single hanger, could now coordinate pants and jackets of different but compatible colors. It seems obvious, but for Syms, which had been selling suits for forty years, it was revolutionary.

Department stores like Saks and Neiman Marcus were already helping men put together sports coats and slacks, instead of the ubiquitous suit, and offices around the country were making announcements that they were adopting casual Friday. It's a short step between casual Friday and casual Monday, Tuesday, Wednesday, and Thursday as well. In the burgeoning tech industry, whose dress code seemed to be black T-shirts and denim, with a crewneck sweater if it got too chilly, nary a suit was to be seen anymore.

For people who had made our fortunes in the suit industry, this was a very difficult change, especially for the manufacturers to adjust their production. There were several years where manufacturers offered us more name-brand men's suits than we could physically house and sell before they went out of fashion.

The hope was that we could attract a younger male customer who had the self-confidence to buy their suit separates at Syms.

As we continued to adjust to falling suit sales, we were putting more resources in other areas of merchandising and expanding offerings to children's clothing, housewares, and, of course, the women's department. That effort was difficult, as we now saw many of our regional competitors for women's off-price clothing coming off a very strong decade of the 1990s, having developed brand loyalty from women just as we had for men.

Like any consumer-facing business, we zeroed in on marketing promotion and consumer loyalty. One of my favorite promotions involved preparing materials for university and college seniors on how to prepare your first career wardrobe. We called this *career dressing.* For a young male student, there were five clothing areas. A dark gray or navy blue suit, a blue blazer, gray and khaki pants, three shirts and three ties. Just as Donna Karan had put together the basic shapes of a woman's wardrobe, Syms put together the basic starter kit for a career wardrobe. We still had the biggest selection of sizes at the best prices.

We put together a visual and written presentation, in the form of a pamphlet and then, through stores managers and marketing people, contacted universities in our markets. We were able to entice one of my brothers, who had occasionally done commercials, to be the spokesperson for this campaign, and he really enjoyed presenting to college seniors. As much as this was a labor of love, it was a very slow and arduous way for a national brand to develop the younger demographic market. Eventually we gave up on it.

Instead, we took it to the internet. To further entice college-age consumers to the website, we started doing what had long been forbidden at Syms—coupons—in this case, online coupons. To Syms veterans it was as if we had invited the fox into the henhouse. Our pricing structure wasn't set up for this extra layer of markdowns. It required everyone to become much more protective of their initial markups in order to leave room for profit at the end.

While we were creatively taking on different ways to introduce ourselves to a broader market, our competitors were doing exactly the same thing. Many of them had migrated to discount economics away from off-price and so it seemed were more agile at adapting their profitability to deep discount promotions. For a time we offered to match any lower price a customer found elsewhere on the same item. This was our core promise to our customers—we told them they were getting the best value at Syms, always.

In fact, we didn't get many customers bringing in sales receipts or newspaper ads showing lower prices elsewhere. In part this was because we kept our eyes open, with managers visiting competitors at least once a week to do comparison shopping. We knew what they were up to. It was part of our culture. But we'd never before given the consumer the idea that we were fallible and might have a higher price.

In the 2000s, I started seeing more regularity in our business. We were no longer the first mover, and we no longer led the go-go growing retail market. It was now a fight to maintain market share. This very much changed the excitement level.

The passing of my brother Stephen in 1998, and the passing of my younger sister Adrienne in 1999, noticeably affected Sy's pleasure in life overall, and he seemed to pull back a little on wanting to try new things.

I was sensing a real transition from Sy to me. I had been named CEO, and while we had in writing lines of authority, responsibilities, and goals for each other, we shared this document and I annoyingly reviewed and revised it every year. Sy admired me for spending all this time writing this down— he thought everything important could fit on a 3-by-5 file card—but he didn't pay much attention to it. I got the feeling ultimately that I was not understanding what he was living through, the aging process and the process of going over his life in his mind.

He was doing more and more self-examination as it seemed life was moving too quickly for him. The indignity of aging was apparent. It forced him to face his own mortality. Because of his heart disease, he had stents put in. As his daughter and someone who deeply loved him, I was there for him and prodded him to take a day off from time to time.

The aging of the founding generation is a challenge for any family business. It's very tricky when the older generation no longer has the creative juices that were always so abundant.

We had previously all seen a family business therapist (yes, that's a thing—87 percent of US businesses are family owned, by far the biggest share). Because of my speaking and thinking about family businesses, my book and my magazine column, I had a lot of contacts.

I suggested to Sy it might be a good idea to get some sort of formatting for the transition with an outside consultant. We hired someone, and the first meeting was at a hotel in the Hamptons. My sister, two of my brothers, and I talked Saturday evening and all day Sunday about our expectations as Sy's offspring.

I thought it was positive. It was an opportunity to have a trained professional listening and nudging our discussion. Sy wasn't so favorably inclined. We had only two more meetings at our distribution center in Secaucus. After our last session I talked to the therapist.

He told me, "Your father owns the stage, has written the play, and he's the producer. He's not comfortable with other roles."

So where does that leave me being able to do things? I thought. But I also thought that this was not a bad thing to have confirmed. It reinforced my observation and it was a real reckoning to hear it from someone who dealt with a lot of founders.

Through the 2000s I modulated expectations of where I could be the most effective. I did this keeping in mind the health of the company, but also the health of my relationship with Sy and my siblings. I consciously tried to take a lot of pressure off myself. I had a young child and was juggling lots of outside speaking invitations and boards of directors offers.

Still, I was able to do more than I had done in previous decades and enjoyed it more. It increased influence for the company and provided it with what I uniquely could do.

I took the lead, for example, in representing Syms and our industry in a battle to have Congress pass a law to undo the likely catastrophic effects of a Supreme Court decision in 2007.

The Court ruled in *Leegin Creative Leather Products, Inc. vs. PSKS, Inc.* that manufacturers could set a minimum retail price for the goods they made—a decision that would potentially limit all of our ability to offer the low prices that were our lifeblood.

Our cause was championed in Congress by Senator Herb Kohl, Democrat of Wisconsin, of the family-owned Kohl's department store chain. We couldn't have dreamed of a better advocate. He and his staff drafted a bill, the Discount Pricing Consumer Protection Act, which would allow retailers to charge whatever they wanted.

I was honored to testify at a hearing on Senator Kohl's bill that would basically outlaw so-called retail price maintenance agreements, (RPMs) and let us charge whatever we felt it took to move the goods. My testimony was on July 31, 2007. The bill finally became law three years later.

While pointing out that I was neither a lawyer nor an economist, I outlined six major problems I saw with restoring the RPMs. First, limiting price flexibility would interfere with consumer choice. Second, they might lead manufacturers to illegally fix prices. Third, it might restrict end-of-season pricing, traditionally heavily discounted. Fourth, it might give foreign retailers, not subject to the RPMs, an advantage. Fifth, retailers would incur increased transaction costs by having to comply with new rules. Finally, RPMs would limit the ability of off-price retailers like Syms to grow in an already tough market.

While my testimony was one voice, it was one voice among many. When the bill finally passed, Senator Kohl acknowledged that pressure from both small and large retailers was important in counteracting a pressure campaign from manufacturers demanding an end to discounting.

I found this episode to be a perfect encapsulation of how when government works and representatives have their constituents' interests first and foremost as their priorities, things that affect our lives can be smoothed out by principled public servants. Herb was doing exactly what a senator should do to help consumers and retailers. This doesn't happen nearly often enough.

We were subjected to competition from right and left. With computers and the internet coming into people's homes, it was becoming harder and harder for us to grow simply by opening more stores in more places. In addition, we were proudly a unionized company with mostly nonunionized competitors.

Sy used to say growing fast covers up a multitude of issues. But when you stop growing, those issues stare you in the face. That's what I was up against.

We always respected differences in the buying power of customers in Houston vs., say, Boston. People had different tastes and spending habits. So we didn't make cookie-cutter, one-size-fits-all decisions. Our managers had a lot of flexibility.

Despite this flexibility, it turned out we weren't flexible enough when we tried to acquire our way to major growth.

CHAPTER 11

Filene's and the Beginning of the End

A woman is like a tea bag. You don't know her strength
until she gets in hot water.
—attributed to Eleanor Roosevelt

In 1999, we were approached by the owners of Filene's Basement, an off-price retailer right in our lane, about acquiring the company, which was then seeking to come out of bankruptcy after an ill-advised expansion. We didn't do the deal then because the stores were mainly in bad repair. We didn't want to take on the huge expense of bringing them up to our standards.

Still, they were a tough competitor and used many of our techniques, including automatic markdowns, in their stores.

Over the next ten years they were acquired by Retail Ventures, Jay Schottenstein's holding company for the DSW shoe chain. He put a lot of money into redoing the stores, and by 2009 they were beautiful—maybe too beautiful for off-price stores (remember Syms's black interiors?) and stocked with high-quality merchandise, much of it from his importing company.

When they came back to us in 2009, again during a bankruptcy, we listened. They were a great fit for us and to be honest, the 2000s had been rough for all of us. We were in a pitched battle for men's sales with Men's Wearhouse and while still profitable, we were losing market share and had no more tricks up our sleeve.

They approached us in March and negotiations dragged on through the bankruptcy proceedings in Delaware. In July our lawyers, Lowenstein Sandler, produced a mammoth leather-bound book consisting of legalese and hundreds upon hundreds of pages of lists of Filene's real property, leases, assets, and the like. We had "won." The bankruptcy judge awarded the entity of Filene's Basement to Syms.

The story turned out to be that the company wasn't in as good shape as it seemed, and nothing we could bring to it, especially in the rapidly changing retail market, could save the combined entity.

It didn't help that about the same time, Sy was visibly declining. He passed away November 17, 2009, just months after we closed the deal. He had been an enthusiastic advocate for it, which in retrospect is one of the reasons I had gone ahead with it.

My due diligence had clearly shown a difference in our corporate cultures, which to my eternal regret I chose to downplay. We were fiscally conservative—pay as you go, fund expansion from profits. They funded it from debt. We'd have sandwiches in the stores for our staff meetings. They went out to lunch at fancy restaurants. They had a corporate jet. We had a few cars.

I was eventually persuaded—wrongly, as it turned out—that our customer demographics were similar and we both had the same message for our customers: they all felt they got great deals. There were definite buying synergies and both sides felt it was great for the industry to have a bigger buyer for name-brand overruns. Besides, it only cost us $63 million, easily funded.

On paper this was a dream deal for Syms. Sy thought it would help us with younger women, an area where, despite

Marcy's Place and everything else, we were still behind the competition. And it would be a poke in the eye to Men's Wearhouse, who was also bidding for Filene's.

We would be extending the life of Filene's, a place where I had shopped while in school in Boston. The economics seemed quite digestible. We got a revolving loan and found a couple of banks willing to extend additional lines of credit with inventory as collateral.

There was a lot of celebrating after the deal closed. These were two historic, venerable names, known and beloved in their markets and a key part of the clothing industry for fifty years. I felt joy at saving Filene's name, jubilation that Filene's would be an ongoing business, not just a website. I was proud that it gave Sy hope for the future. His own and the company's.

At a party at the Metropolitan Club in New York on August 17, 2009, just after the closing, a group of well-lubricated Syms executives wrote and recited a poem entitled "The Night Before Closing," after Clement Clarke Moore's "A Visit from St. Nicholas." It started out:

It was a day back in March, I think it was Tuesday,
I had a strange call from Houlihan Lokey.
'Twas said that Filene's was looking to be bought.
Would we like to look and would we give it some
thought?

It was a clever celebration of all we'd been through and achieved.

Combining the two companies involved a headache-inducing number of meetings, but also some fun. Early on we took top management to the Mohegan Sun resort in Connecticut for the weekend. We had stickers, films, motivational speakers, prizes, team-building exercises, the lot. At Syms we tended to build teams in the store, without all this, but we gave it a concerted try. After all, as management guru Peter Drucker famously said, "Culture eats strategy for breakfast."

One perfect fit for us was Filene's annual Running of the Brides event, which spawned a made-for-TV movie in 2008. Held in Boston since 1949, the event featured more than 15,000 square feet of selling space filled with wedding gowns and bridal accessories. In this one-day sale, you might find a $2,000 wedding gown for $299. Women came with their bridesmaids, sisters, mothers, and friends to sift through the goods amid the hundreds of brides—elbows out—and try the dresses on in the aisles.

This was no-frills and very Syms-like in the direct-to-customer appeal and nontraditional pricing.

I had an affection for Filene's, even though department store culture was different than off-price culture. I wanted to combine the stores—we had thirty-seven Syms stores and twenty Filene's Basement stores—and all the inventory.

Here's where we were, according to SEC filings:

> The Company converted four former Syms stores (Norwood, MA, Berlin, CT, Elmsford, NY and Westbury, NY) to co-branded stores in fiscal 2010. In fiscal 2009, the Company converted one former Syms store (Fairfield, CT) to a co-branded store. These stores carry the names of both Syms and Filene's Basement and combine the strengths of both brands with an expanded selection of women's merchandise in the former Syms stores. We continue to monitor the customer reaction and store performance; at present, no additional locations have been identified for co-branding for fiscal 2011.

As of February 26, 2011, the Company had approximately 2,500 employees, of which approximately 1,400 work on a part-time basis. Each store employs anywhere from approximately 30 to 160 associates, consisting mostly of sales personnel. Syms has collective bargaining agreements with Local 1102 and Local 108, both of the Retail Wholesale Department Store Workers Union (RWDSU). Syms also has a collective bargaining agreement with Local 400 of the United Food and Commercial Workers Union. In 2010, the majority of Filene's Basement store employees voted to be represented by RWDSU Local 1102. A new agreement was negotiated which covers approximately 1,100 Filene's Basement store employees and expires on June 21, 2012. The Company believes that its relationship with its unions and employees is good.

One of the main reasons we bought Filene's was to improve our position with women and on that front, it worked. The chart below shows women's sales overtaking men's for the first time in our history.

Merchandise for fiscal 2010, net sales were generated by the following categories:	
Women's dresses, suits, separates and accessories	46%
Men's tailored clothes and haberdashery	38%
Children's apparel	5%
Luggage, domestics and fragrances	6%
Shoes	5%

Most of the items sold by the Company consist of nationally recognized designer and brand-name merchandise. Merchandise is generally displayed by department, class and size on conveniently arranged racks, fixtures, tables or counters. No emphasis is placed on any particular "label" or brand. Most stores offer minor alterations for an additional charge.

We took a Syms store we had built ourselves in Norwalk, Connecticut, with 75,000 square feet of selling space, and decided to reengineer, re-sign, and work as a laboratory experiment on how we might present merchandise under a fully integrated Syms-Filene offering. We even designed a beautiful new, two-name logo that went on everything from signage to carrier bags.

We even made a video mashing together a few Syms ads with my dad and I giving our spiel, with a Filene's ad showing a young mother pushing a baby carriage and gushing over all the bargains she had just found at Filene's, piled where the baby should be.

A lot of Filene's merchandise was planned, ordered at the beginning of the seasons from manufacturers, designed by famous designers including Linda Allard, Ellen Tracy, or Josephine Chaus. These were solid middle-market brands that had created a stylistic following and gave style positioning to Filene's for skirts, sweaters, and blouses. Since Filene's controlled the manufacturing of these brands, they also controlled the pricing, which was often higher than Syms's for similar goods.

But most of all, it gave them consistent availability of size, color, and style. They made all they needed the seasons before, just like a department store, but unlike Syms, which feasted off of leftovers.

I was anxious to bring Filene's advantages to Syms's women

customers. In the combined stores, the men's department was all Syms. But the women's department was a hybrid, adding their brands to ours. Besides the joint labels with both names and the signage and bags, we redesigned the price tickets and gave the entire store a facelift. Suddenly, there were brighter colors and non-black walls. This was a chance to reposition us for the future. It was a rebirth and very exciting.

Even some of the hedge funds saw this as an opportunity for us to grow our retail operations.

The Norwalk experiment was a success, so we started rolling it out to other locations in Connecticut and Rhode Island. We did some modest addition of Filene's goods to our Union Square store in New York City and got some negative pushback from customers. Men complained there wasn't as good a selection as there was at Syms downtown at Trinity Place, but that wasn't true. There was an enormous selection of more than 400 brands at both locations. I guess people were just used to what they were used to. I even got a complaint about our new signs, which were computer generated. The old signs had all been hand-painted. Some of this was psychological. "You changed my Syms!"

After we combined five stores in six months, I hit the brake pedal. I said we had to assess how this would work in all our various demographic markets and look at sales after eighteen months.

Overall, the enthusiasm within the company for the merger was high. We lost some people, especially the Filene's buyers. I admit having a bias toward Syms buyers, but we did keep several Filene's buyers. The store managers generally stayed in place, and the Filene's people always told us they were glad that Men's Wearhouse hadn't bought them.

In 2010, I got an award as Retailer of the Year from the Manhattan Chamber of Commerce. The award was for saving jobs, reviving two venerable brands, maintaining the leases, and expanding. When I accepted the award in late spring, I already knew there was a problem. It was difficult. It caused me great internal distress that I couldn't say anything. When we listed the combined company on the Nasdaq exchange, I got to ring the opening bell. We were still smiling and working hard.

What happened? There's an old adage that in doing a deal, you never want to be the smaller fish. Professionals all know the next deal will come from the big fish, not you. We were the smaller fish and we got swallowed.

In hindsight, I had some warning that all might not be as it seemed. During the negotiations I met with Filene's people a lot.

During one meeting early on in the talks, I had gone to the ladies' room outside the conference room. Upon exiting, I saw one of the executives waiting for me outside the room.

He said, "Why didn't you walk away?"

I said, "Why should I?"

"Because you could lose everything."

This memory still gives me shivers. We could have walked away and let Men's Wearhouse buy Filene's Basement. We all would probably have ended up going out of business, as we later did, but it would've saved me and Syms stakeholders a lot of money and aggravation.

As soon as we closed on Filene's, challenges emerged. One was the fact that we were a union shop and they weren't, so the union needed to organize all of their stores under the same locals. It took time and left some grudges.

We thought our Syms culture was so strong, and correct, because we'd all learned to bleed Syms. It provided our livelihoods and fed our families.

Once we began trying to integrate the Filene's workforce, we found that the culture didn't seem to be transferable. They were glamorous, we were Brooklyn. They spent on things we called frills. They loved those long lunches and long meetings. You can take the company out of Brooklyn, but you can't take Brooklyn out of the company.

I thought they'd all sign on to our value system, but it didn't happen.

Management from executive suite to the selling floors loved the hotel suites and private jets. They were never really measured on performance as closely as we did. Above all, they benefited from top management always riding in at the end of the day, or the quarter, and making it all right through accounting changes.

As for the accounting, there was one major lingering question, one that I kick myself to this day for not getting answered before closing: Why hadn't Filene's produced audited financials signed off by their auditors? They kept giving excuses and assurances, but never produced them.

When we finally got more information from their auditors, though never a fully verified set of books—they said that wasn't possible with the information they had from Filene's—the statute of limitations on any fraud accusations in New York State had lapsed, and there was nothing legally we could do.

> Cautionary tale: Don't invest so much emotionally and financially in a deal that you can't walk away. Always be prepared to drop it.

Six months in, I got nervous and told the board there was something odd going on. This was in itself a difficult economic time. Lehman Brothers had collapsed, threatening to take the whole financial system with it. The great recession was in full swing. Consumers weren't consuming. Jobs were being lost left and right.

The market was developing in ways we hadn't foreseen,

and it was moving fast. Internet shopping grew exponentially. Amazon and others were figuring out how to deliver virtually anything you wanted right to your house in a couple of days, and these days even quicker. Casual clothes were taking over even before the pandemic cemented their triumph. China had figured out how to make decent quality clothes at costs below what we could offer for irregulars.

Starting in 2007, hedge funds had become more vocal. Activist shareholders, who had been around since the 1980s, took on a new face: richly capitalized hedge funds. Carl Ichan led the most notable one, but there were a lot of copycats who wanted to make a name and differentiate themselves by creating a very aggressive position on stocks they believed were undervalued.

By buying 5 percent of a company's shares, the funds or any other shareholder had to make an SEC filing and state their investment purpose. This was often to pressure the management to cut costs or improve earnings or raise the dividend, or to demand positions on the board.

That started happening to us in 2007. I found myself spending a great deal more time on shareholder relations, lawyers, and communicating to financial markets than ever. The inclusion in my focus of the constant consideration of how they would react to anything I did was distracting. They started dumping negative articles about our company at 4 p.m. on Fridays, often in the *New York Post*.

One such on Friday, May 27, 2011, was headed SIMMERING SYMS and said unnamed investors were "fretting" that I was going to somehow make off with all the cash because I had hired investment bankers to try to sell the company as a whole, rather than break off chunks and sell them for the real estate, which was what the funds and their backers implied they wanted.

A lurking fear among some investors is that the company's chief, daughter of the late founder Sy Syms, is angling to find a fi-

nancial partner to help her take the retailer private before pursu-
ing a lucrative strategy to capitalize on the value of Syms' properties.

It wasn't true, but then again neither were dozens of other such stories.

The very thing that made us more valuable and durable as a retailer, being our own landlord and owning our buildings, was the thing that made us so attractive to raiders. Because of our land and buildings, we were more valuable dead than alive.

It was easy to get appraisals for our real estate; our more than twenty properties held lots of value. The hedge funds figured it out and started a relentless drive toward ending the retail business, which wasn't showing enough return on equity to satisfy them.

In October 2010, a little more than a year after the closing, I called an emergency board meeting and said we needed to hire investment bankers and examine alternative strategies. All code words for *bankruptcy* and *reorganization*.

As the leader, 1 took full responsibility for the mess we were in and for trying to get out of it with the best possible result for all of our stakeholders. Sy had always told me that if you're the leader of the company, you have to have broad shoulders, because a lot is resting on them.

My shoulders were up to the task, but the rest of me was a mess. I developed irritable bowel syndrome, hives, and lost twenty pounds.

Worse was yet to come.

CHAPTER 12

Getting Reorganized

Just because you make a good plan doesn't mean that's what's gonna happen.
—Taylor Swift

A s we filed for reorganization, I issued a statement explaining our reasons. "Increased competition from large department stores that now offer the same brands as our stores at similar discounts; a proliferation of private label discount chains; a decline in buying opportunities as brand name labels have reduced overruns by improving their supply chain management—all combined with the worst economic downturn in our lifetimes."

I still believe those were the main factors behind the need for the reorganization. I remain wistful for the past shopping pleasures, and I did what I could to get a fair shake for those who lost their jobs.

I never sold out or compromised my values. We managed to get a fair deal for employees, shareholders, and vendors by getting what we could for the valuable real estate the stores sat upon.

The closure of the physical stores was met with anger in some quarters, but genuine regret and nostalgia in others. One of my favorite articles of the time was a *Washington Post* opinion column by Annie Greer on December 30, 2011, entitled "The Filenes-Basement-Going-Out-Of-Business Blues."

By Jan. 1, after more than a century as a department store and then as a famous off-price clothier, all 21 remaining Basements plus 25 sibling Syms stores will have gone dark, throwing 2,500 people out of work, mostly on the East Coast.

In recent days, equally bummed Syms regulars bid fond farewell to the staff at the Rockville and Falls Church stores. "It's like it was a funeral," mused Linda Mock, who'd worked at Syms stores in Virginia for 33 years . . .

I also feel for Marcy Syms, chief executive of the eponymous empire founded by her father, Sy, in 1959. "Syms, where an educated consumer is our best customer," the two would kvell in TV ads touting their high-end, low-price wares.

In June 2009, five months before Sy's death, his daughter acquired Filene's Basement in a federal bankruptcy auction, betting that the two stores' long retail history and consumer brand loyalty could carry the day. Alas, two months ago, Marcy—I call her by her first name because, frankly, she feels like a longtime shopping girl-friend—blamed this latest Chapter 11 ordeal on three factors: less good stuff from suppliers, more rivals and a killer recession.

Less kind, predictably, was the *New York Post*, which once ran a bizarre, doctored picture of me in a cat suit climbing a skyscraper. I forget why. After the filing, their headline was THE SYMS SAGA: FROM RAGS TO RICHES TO RAGS and they called us "tattered off-price clothing chains."

After the emergency board meeting in October 2010, everything seemed to go wrong, and it looked like we were going down quickly.

In order to put a team together that was able to assess the situation and make recommendations to the board on alternate strategic options for the Syms-Filene's company, we hired an investment banker to help us manage and present the alternatives to the board and ultimately to the public shareholders. One of the outside advisers was the consulting firm of Alvarez & Marsal.

Without being prepared in any way for what was to come, I had to make a decision about putting a partner from Alvarez into our offices, along with one of their accountants, who would be acting as an outside pair of eyes, kind of a pseudo-CFO. I had done my due diligence. I had also met with other firms that did this kind of work, and felt that Tony Alvarez, a founding partner, was very easy to talk with and didn't mind spending a lot of time with me, answering questions.

I was soon to interview the person he sent to sit across from me, Jeff Feinberg. Jeff arrived and made it clear from the start that he was going to find information that was going to save money, identify waste, and that this was going to be incontrovertible for me and the organization.

Everyone understood that this was something we wanted to be successful in because we were hoping not to have to go to the courts for a reorganization of our assets. After being on-site for three weeks, with access to anything he wanted, Jeff came into my office and said, "Do you have a minute?" He sat down and showed me in essence that there was no way for us to save money because we were being run very efficiently.

Jeff joked with me, "I can't even go after your expense account, because you rarely use it." I said, "Jeff, I grew up in an off-price business and that's my mindset. I walk the walk."

I felt somewhat vindicated as a CEO for running a tight ship, but I also knew that in the bigger picture, this was not good news for us in trying to create a longer runway in order to figure a way out.

The whole drawn-out process was emotional. I remember specifically a meeting where the ostensible purpose was to discuss the future of our Filene's leases. When the conversation got around to what my future might look like, it was clear to me that I'd have to put my personal goals and lifelong commitments in abeyance, while working things out for all the stakeholders. One of the executives asked me, "Well, what are you gonna do if we have to go through bankruptcy and there's no Syms?"

I remember saying, typically resorting to a Bette Davis/ Joan Crawford voice, "Well, it hasn't been as much fun since my dad died, so I'm not sure I care much." This was a lie. Of course I cared, but I didn't want to give them the satisfaction of showing how much I cared. I'd worked there thirty-five years and helped build the company. This was my extended family. This was my father's legacy. I felt close and protective toward coworkers I had worked side by side with. It was wrenching.

It was important to me that they understood I wasn't going through this long, painful process, being manipulated and insulted, just for concerns about the legacy of my name. The main thing I was concerned about was treating the stockholders as ethically as possible under the circumstances and that Syms and Filene's coworkers got their pensions. I'm pleased to say, even though it took over a year and many personal financial sacrifices, we paid 100 cents on the dollar to all of our Syms creditors, all of our union pension funds stayed whole, and even our landlords (all from Filene's) got 75 cents on every dollar. This is pretty unheard of in Chapter 11 reorganizations. We wound up being reorganized into a publicly traded (on Nasdaq) real estate company (which still exists) and which I was not a part of.

One of the Filene's Basement landlords reached out when things started going south and thought he could help by infusing some money as an investment. We had several meetings, but at the end of the day, after too many meetings, he was just stalling, and as every month went by, I was in a weaker position to accomplish the full credit payback I had hoped to do.

This thug actually threatened my life. I've never been afraid at the moment of a threat, but like many people, I felt it afterwards. I was silent. He growled, "If you're hiding anything I'll find it and I'll track you and your family members down. Your life will be hell."

A thug is a thug is a thug, even if he's wearing a bespoke $3,000 tailored suit (I did admire the suit) and went to the University of Pennsylvania.

I remember thinking, *There's no comeback for this. There are no words to defuse such vitriol. Crazy.* I stayed silent but kept eye contact. I shared the story with my attorney, who calmed me down. He said this is actually normal stuff for these guys. They do it all the time. He would do it to you in the morning and someone else at lunch. Retail was competitive, but nothing like real estate. Respect? Fuggedaboutit!

I became calmer, but his words didn't lessen my concern that someone like this felt he had access to interfere with my life.

During this time, I found it very helpful and sustaining to be able to lean in to some of my good friends who were listening without judging, not hounding me on how things were going every day, because it was impossible to give a daily reading, but were there for the occasional dinner or walk in the park. I trusted their reassurance and love.

My husband was a rock. I couldn't take a day off or go on our planned ski trip to Steamboat Springs with our son. In fact, none of the plans made a year earlier could be fulfilled, but the only thing I ever heard from him was, *I'm here, what do you need.*

Toward the end of this draining process, when we sold some of Syms's real estate and had to go through regulatory issues to use the assets for operations, not creditors, it was time for a big meeting. Jay Goffman of Skadden, Arps was our lead counsel. Jay and I had gotten into the habit of speaking at 7 a.m. each day. Skadden had been our counsel since the 1997 secondary offering. My dear friend Nancy Lieberman, who was their youngest lawyer ever to make partner, was helpful in introducing me to Jay, whose ethics and commitment to workers and not just the C-suite made us compatible teammates.

Jay suggested that we get all the parties—hostile hedge funds, people who wanted the real estate, hedge funds dissing us on Page Six of the *New York Post*—everyone with an iron in the fire. Let's get them in one room and ask the judge to be there so we could hash this out and reach a final deal, so it wouldn't go on and on.

We met in the large conference room at Skadden, Arps's 4 Times Square office. There were fifty-four people in the room, four of whom were women, including me. We met with the judge at various points and with several subgroups. After all the stakeholders had done presentations and aired their beefs and demands, Jay asked me and my personal attorney to go in and speak with the judge.

The moment was an eloquent statement of why the sanctity of the judiciary is so essential to how our society works and how we get along with each other. After some niceties, he said he had shopped at Syms and had enjoyed it.

"What do you think should be done here?"

I shared that the situation was such that the operating business couldn't continue; it needed a reorganization, and my concern was simply that anybody who did business with or worked for us or owned a share of Syms stock should be left with the best possible outcome.

He said, "But what about you, Marcy?"

I said, "Well, I think that's my last consideration. I would like to be part of the ongoing real estate company, but it doesn't seem possible, and if it's not, that's fine with me."

This gave the judge clarity.

As I look back, it's clear I could have been more forceful in seeking a better outcome for myself personally, but this wasn't what I was motivated to want. It was important to me not to leave a legacy of destruction. I wanted to feel I could move on. I wanted Sy to be proud because he was still with me in spirit every step of the way.

After the stores closed, we had looked into strategic alternatives. Working with investment bankers, we'd explored packaging the company in various ways in order to sell it. But coming out of the great recession of 2007–2009, there was little interest in retail companies.

I met with the credit bureau, bankers, and vendors in order to keep flow of inventory coming to the stores, but by end of December 2011, it was clear we needed to close our retail businesses, both Filene's and Syms. Starting on Thanksgiving 2011 we ran the going-out-of-business sales and by the week after Christmas we were selling store furnishings and equipment. By January 2012 it was a matter of sweeping, washing, and polishing because there was nothing left in the buildings.

The thought with me every second of the day was, *Thank God my father didn't live to see this.*

I kept asking myself why we didn't see this coming. I had a terrible sense of failure. I felt I had let down everyone, from

the shareholders to the store cashiers and our loyal customers. Although Sy was 100 percent behind the acquisition, I
was glad he wasn't around to see that it didn't work. How
come, with all the people we had been paying to help us
avoid this outcome, we couldn't avoid it?

In the fullness of time, I can now see that it wasn't all our
fault. The market had completely changed and so had Wall
Street. If Sy thought he was "bad at Wall Street" ten years
previously, he would have been flabbergasted in 2011. With
hedge funds and activist shareholders now focusing on a
small company like ours, it made no sense for us to be trading in the public market.

Our small size actually made us a target because we had
assets—real estate. Vultures feast on this stuff, because they
can strip assets quickly and easily. It felt to me that we were
being picked apart by vultures.

Syms holders now held shares of a real estate investment
company and could still benefit.

I stayed on until June 2012. It was very sad, and I started
every day feeling a little bit like Dorothy in the *Wizard of Oz*,
clicking my heels together and repeating over and over, *You
will get through this, you will get through this.*

In both the Filene's acquisition and the reorganization, I
did the best I could with what was on my plate and tried to
do it with the most qualified professionals we could afford,
and with the full participation of our board every step of
the way.

It was the end of the retail company, but nowhere near the
end of my productive life.

CHAPTER 13

Getting Involved

Discover who you are, and use who you are in service to the world.
—Oprah Winfrey

My introduction to the world of philanthropy, which I've been involved in for more than forty years, started when my dad had emergency heart surgery.

Sy had heart disease, with his first event at age thirty-two. He had a triple bypass when he was fifty-five. Because of that and the heart disease deaths of my brother and sister, we got more involved with the American Heart Association. I went on the board of the New York branch. There I met Dr. Nieca Goldberg and Jane Chesnutt, publisher of *Woman's Day* magazine, who were raising money for research into women's heart disease, a neglected area of study. At that time, there was little understanding of the very different symptoms a woman having a heart attack might display in an emergency room.

Research money from the government and private donations was put into research projects that almost exclusively looked at heart disease symptoms in men. We suggested that because of the difference in symptoms, funds raised would be used only for research into women's symptoms. We started a consumer awareness and fundraising campaign built around the slogan *Go Red* and asking women to wear red scarves to work the first Friday in February. Eventually we were able to get a poster up in every emergency room in the US that showed the specific symptoms of heart attacks in women. It saved countless lives. Still today, heart disease is the number one killer of women, ahead of breast cancer.

Support for this cause became a major Syms corporate effort. We involved all of the stores in our eighteen major markets. We handed out literature and put up *Go Red* posters. If anyone asked for more information, we directed them to the AHA websites. The *Go Red* campaign is still going. Oprah, the women on *The View*, and many others wear red scarves on the first Friday in February.

Today, WHAM (Women's Health Access Matters), a group started by my friend Carolee Lee, is continuing the battle, raising funds that are directed at medical research that uses women and our unique anatomy, chemistry, and aging process to inform pharmaceutical companies and doctors—and of course, our government—why women and men should not get the same prescriptions and certainly not the same diagnoses.

During the mid-1990s a woman, with whom I had done work with on family business, had a daughter who was doing something really unique for the time. The daughter, Rosalind Wiseman, had organized self-defense classes and had convinced a school to let her teach girls self-defense. She focused on the very tumultuous middle school ages, a time when girls often stop trying so hard at school and become extremely self-critical about their appearance.

Rosalind came to me with the idea of expanding these self-defense classes, and we hit it off right away. Ross, as she today refers to herself, had such a powerful perspective on the need to nurture adolescent girls on the skills they would need to become future CEOs. She later wrote the book *Queen Bees and Wannabes*, which was the basis for the movie *Mean Girls*.

One of my favorite causes was called Bottomless Closet. This is an organization—still going strong—dedicated to helping disadvantaged women dress properly in order to make a good impression while job-seeking. It checked all my boxes.

When they gave me an award, I told them why they were so important:

> Think of your very first job interview—how much of your hopes and dreams were riding on the first impression you would make. Multiply that by tenfold and you can, for a moment, walk in the shoes of a client of Bottomless Closet.
>
> Making money is serious business—there's nothing "corporate casual" about it! First impressions on a job interview can determine the outcome more than the substance of the interview.
>
> Just imagine you have a job interview tomorrow at noon. You need to prepare a résumé, put an appropriate outfit together, and arrange for childcare in order to be there on time. Now also imagine that you are desperately trying to get off welfare.
>
> With a combination of personal shopper, image consultant, and job counseling service, Bottomless Closet's reason for being is to turn those judgment points during an interview into an opportunity to make the best first impression, every time.
>
> All of us, no matter how much success or recognition we receive, sometimes need a helping hand. We must recognize opportunity and respond to it when it knocks on our door. We must be ready to offer positive impressions to the right opportunities.

Many of my later involvements were while I was working for Syms, but required time commitments mostly outside of my fifty-hour work week. It was the presence of my face on

TV and my voice on the radio that made my name pop up when organizations in need of building their own awareness campaigns reached out to me. If I believed in the mission and had the time, I was usually inclined to say yes. I also represented the company Syms in many of these nonprofit efforts.

I met Elinor Guggenheimer at WMCA in 1977, before I started at Syms. Elinor had a show called *Call for Action* on WMCA, working with Ellen Straus, Peter's wife. Elinor later became New York City's Consumer Affairs Commissioner, the first woman in the post. She was a strong voice for me, and one of the founders of the New York Women's Forum, which I joined. When I started working for Syms, Elinor was a mentor and an example of what one can accomplish without having a big corporation behind you, as an activist and organizer. She was so creative about engaging people and making them feel appreciated.

She showed me that having a platform, as I did, made it even more important for me to do philanthropic works. I saw that improving the lives of women would improve everyone's life in a family. That's what I devoted myself to.

Underlying everything is trying to say yes whenever you can. You never know where it's going to wind up a couple of years later.

Early on during my time at Syms, a woman reached out from a start-up organization called Executive Women of New Jersey, asking me to join them. I said yes. One thing led to another and they put me on their list of potential board members. That led to my being asked to serve on the board of Midlantic Bank, since acquired by PNC Bank.

This was the first of several serial connections. I was their first female board member, and a couple of years later they wanted to give me an award. My dad always said of these events, "Don't get too impressed with yourself. They want the company to buy some tables at the awards dinner."

Anyway, Sy agreed to present me with the award. But at the last minute, he had to cancel. The substitute presenter was Muriel Siebert, the first woman to own a seat on the New York Stock Exchange. I was very grateful she was willing to step in at such short notice, and we became friendly after the event. She was a generous role model and mentor until her death in 2013.

The next connection happened at her funeral. I happened to be sitting next to Representative Carolyn Maloney, who I knew and supported. We chatted about what I had been doing on boards and foundations, and she pointed her finger at me and said, "I have something for you."

That something was the ERA Coalition, an effort to bring together all the activists who had been working on the Equal Rights Amendment. The ERA was first introduced in Congress in 1923, but wasn't passed by both chambers until 1972. It was ratified by thirty-five of the necessary thirty-eight states, but those last three needed to satisfy Article Five and amend the Constitution were missing. The challenge was to mobilize opinion in three more states for ratification, and to deal with the complication that Congress had set a long-passed deadline for ratification, and a few states had rescinded their original ratification.

This sounded perfect to me. I made a few calls, had a few meetings, put some money into the Fund for Women's Equality, and was off and running.

After working on the ERA coalition, I was surprised and delighted to receive the Woman of Vision award from *Ms.* magazine in 2016. It gave me great motivation to continue doing the thankless job of organizing and educating for social change. *Ms.*'s audience is all about equal rights for women and, more broadly, gender equality.

In January 2020, Virginia (following Illinois and Nevada), became the thirty-eighth state to ratify the ERA. I left the coalition, but a few months later helped establish the ERA Project.

We're still working. This work needs a home, and it has one in my heart, mind, and pocketbook.

The lesson in all this is that if you say yes, it can lead to incredible places. I look back at that first request to join the start-up women's group that led to the bank board that led to Muriel Siebert that led to Carolyn Maloney at the funeral that led to my work on the ERA, and I'm amazed.

Saying yes opens universes.

I have always loved to make lists. I used them constantly to keep track of what I had to do each day. I also used them both lightheartedly and seriously in speeches to make points about the role of women in society.

Here's one in the style of David Letterman:

The top ten things only women understand:

10. Why it's good to have six pairs of black shoes.
9. The difference between cream, ivory, off-white, and bone.
8. Crying can be fun.
7. FAT clothes.
6. A salad, diet drink, and chocolate cheesecake make a balanced lunch.
5. Why discovering a designer dress at final markdown in Syms can be considered a peak life experience.
4. The inaccuracy of every bathroom scale.
3. A good man might be hard to find, but a good hairdresser is next to impossible.
2. Why a phone call between two women never lasts under 10 minutes.

And the number 1 thing that women understand . . . OTHER WOMEN

In the spring of 2024 I was asked to deliver a brief re-membrance of Elinor to the New York Women's Forum. This is what I said:

> In 1977 I met Elly when I was assistant to R. Peter Straus, the President of WMCA radio, my first job after grad school. Elly was Commissioner of Consumer Affairs and had a weekly listener call-in program called Call for Action.
>
> In the control room listening and watching that first time it was immediately apparent that Elly was plugged-in, driven, charming, competent, and witty. She handled each caller with just a touch of empathy and a lot of cheerleading. Each call ended with a "to-do plan."
>
> Elly's command of the city's civics was a how-to handbook of city politics and networks. There wasn't a part of the city that she didn't have covered in her Rolodex. Almost a decade later, when I was COO and President of Syms, our paths crossed again and we bonded over Democratic politics. She entered my life for keeps this time. Elly was a role model. She showed me it was shameful not to use a platform. It presented opportunity and responsibility. In her role as social entrepreneur, Elly could mobilize and inspire others to her vision. I could never say no to Elly. Who could?

Some of my activism also helped the stores. Our appetite to help the community extended to store managers, who would survey educators and staff and could choose their own causes in their own communities. The goal was to engage and inspire their coworkers and feel proud and engaged and helping their communities.

Syms was an early backer of the Juvenile Diabetes Research Foundation, long fronted by the late Mary Tyler Moore. If you're part of a community, you want more healthy customers and you want to help keep them healthy.

One cause that nicely married my communication background and the stores' need for marketing was our longtime support for public television and NPR.

I got involved with WNET in New York in 1978, my first year at Syms. One of the first tasks I assigned myself was to do a survey of what TV channels (there weren't very many then) our customers watched, so we'd know where best to place our ads.

The Nielsen data was too vague. Our customers knew what they wanted to watch: public TV essentially tied for third place with ABC. Back then you couldn't buy an ad spot on WNET, but you could be creative. I went up there and met with them and decided to try something we're still involved with nearly fifty years later. We put together Movie Night for WNET and did joint advertising with them as sponsor. They'd maybe show six Marlene Dietrich or Greta Garbo movies in a row. Its successor, *Reel 13*, is still sponsored by the Syms Foundation. We also backed *Agronsky & Co.*, which morphed into *Inside Washington*, and *Frontline*. Their viewers were our educated consumers.

Around 2013, after I was no longer involved with the transition to a real estate company, I had the opportunity to turn my attentions careerwise to philanthropy. I was on the board of the Sy Syms Foundation, started in 1985 but funded by the 1983 public offering and the 1997 secondary offering, the "chips" Sy took off the table.

One of the first and longest lasting (it's still going strong) engagements was with the Sy Syms School of Business at Yeshiva University in New York City. Sy had always found it ironic that the largest Jewish university in the country, smack in the heart of a venerable and thriving Jewish business community, had no business school.

He met and was taken with Rabbi Dr. Norman Lamm, YU's president, himself an expert on modern Jewish life and the diaspora. Dr. Lamm was also a native of Brooklyn and a first-generation American who was Sy's age. I was all for investing in this institution and I've never changed my mind. What started with an accounting class of twenty-four students in 1987 is now a fully fledged school with nearly a thousand students and courses on finance and Jewish values, an institute for entrepreneurship, and most importantly the ethics required to do business sustainably.

I recently rewatched a lecture my dad gave in 1995 at the SSSB. In answering student questions, he traced the whole Syms story from lower Manhattan to national prominence, and he must have used the word *respect* twenty-five times in the two hours. It was that central to his worldview and his beliefs around good business practices.

"When you walk in my shop door, I must transmit that I respect you. We want respect to come out in every facet. Our respect for our customers is what drives our profits. Whatever you do, never forget the importance of respect."

The kids got it. They weren't always shown respect in the broader community, but they always gave it because they were taught about its central role in building lasting relationships.

I enjoyed working with Sy on the school. I've often lectured and spoken there and have been honored by the school. Once I was no longer involved in running Syms, I enjoyed being part of search committees for a new president and dean, helping them raise money, and the most joyful part, talking with the students.

Noam Wasserman, the current dean, reflected recently that the school, which boasts a bust of Sy on its main floor, truly reflects the ethics and need for respect that Sy always preached.

"There is a direct line from Sy's start-up story, which everyone here learns, to the ethics and importance of accuracy and respect in management that we teach here. The kids get a unique education, in large part because of his influence."

I'm proud of the business school, which has undergraduate and graduate courses leading to a master's in business, as well as a growing online component. While many of the students come from religious Jewish backgrounds, enrollment is open to everyone.

I'm also proud of my Jewish heritage and was honored to be inducted into the Manhattan Jewish Hall of Fame in 2024, joining such luminaries as actor Debra Messing, sexpert Dr. Ruth Westheimer, first amendment lawyer Floyd Abrams, and actor Joel Grey.

I particularly love the entrepreneurial aspect of philanthropy. I love the energy and challenge of the start-up. You need to define your purpose, your customer base, as it were, and your strategy. It does not necessarily have to be from scratch. As was the case with the Go Red campaign at the American Heart Association—you can become active either with a contribution or by volunteering on a particular cause, such as women's heart health.

Another example is my work for the Weizmann Institute, Israel's world-class research institution. They need more women scientists and that's where I've put my time, money, and contacts. In addition to writing them a check, I opened my *contacts* file and suggested this was an idea they should focus on and develop.

This kind of activity is sometimes called *intrapreneuring*. You take something that already exists and bring a new idea or initiative to the organization via a commitment in time, capital, and other resources, not the least of which is networking capabilities.

Sometimes you get involved because you just love something. I was for many years on the board of the Manhattan

Theatre Club. I love theater and have been an investor in film and theater production. It is hard to think of this as investing since I have not been on the receiving end of any returns, but I always equated these investments with supporting the arts and getting a message out there.

I was flattered to be invited on the MTC board and served for twelve years. I happily chaired their fundraising gala each year, but there came a time when I basically exhausted my contacts. At a certain point any nonprofit needs new blood and new people exposed and connected to new networks. You need to identify new people with a sweet spot for the organization and its mission and goals.

One of my notable investments around that time was in *Other People's Money,* a 1991 film that starred Danny DeVito as a corporate raider breaking up small companies and was Gregory Peck's last film. Did I have some sort of premonition about what was going to happen to us?

I never invested with any expectation that I'd get my money back. I looked for important messages and unique ways of highlighting them. More recently, I've been involved in a not-for-profit Jewish film production company called Jewish Story Partners that seeks to portray complicated issues in a more empathetic light. Several of our films have now been seen at film festivals around the country.

Even though it seems my philanthropy has involved a lot of disparate causes—including women's empowerment, social justice, and civics education and the centrality of civil society—the string that ties them together is respect. I tried to spend my time and money in ways that create a better, fairer, and more well-functioning society.

I also tried to keep my focus at home. As much as I emotionally and intellectually admire those who work on the world stage, I've felt strongly I need focus on my community, my state, and my country, where I think I understand the culture. I try not to be rigidly dogmatic about anything other than trying to treat others as I would like to be treated. This was a core tenet of mine at Syms—respect, if you will—and I like to think it continues to drive me.

Recently, I joined the Lincoln Project as a cohost at a fundraiser. As a lifelong Democrat but not into dogmas, I still felt a bit odd among all the Republicans and ex-Republicans. In these times, politics needs to be transparent and fluid, an overlapping of circles. People say it's a small world and that you travel in small circles, but need to spread your circles out—it's always reenergized me to be part of overlapping circles.

In an odd way, our family's devotion to philanthropy helped my career. In 1991 and 1992, just as we were expanding under our joint leadership, Sy became the national head of Israel Bonds, a major commitment of his time. "Marcy," he said, "I want to clear something with you. I'm gonna be traveling a lot and we'll need to work on our calendars." Israel Bonds was then helping to fund airlifts of Ethiopian and Russian Jews to Israel. He did some great work for them. He also left me with the keys to the kingdom, which I used to implement some of my ideas for Syms.

Over the years I received many awards from organizations we supported. One I'm proudest of came in 2017 from PEN America: their Freedom of Expression Courage Award for work I did on that year's women's march.

I was also proud to receive the Marvin Feldman Award from one of my alma maters, the Fashion Institute of Technology, in 1997. I was the first woman to receive this award, given to a distinguished graduate.

In whatever I did, I was always aware of protecting free speech and writers and a free press, therefore protecting our democracy. There is no democracy without a free press that is balanced and able to support the facts it reports. This belief was so important to me that in 2020 the Sy Syms Foundation endowed the U.S. Free Expression Program at PEN America. This initiative helps push back against book banning and supports the mission of libraries.

Also, in 2020 we worked with the Tanenbaum foundation to support efforts to end bullying in schools, a subject dear to my heart. We endowed a long-term anti-bullying program for public school teachers. I understood the repercussions of bullying on growth, personality, and sense of confidence. At an early age, even in grade school, these kinds of experiences alter trust in one's environment, change the way you engage, and affect your learning capabilities. This program has continued to grow.

After I left Syms, I had the opportunity to become engaged with foundation work full-time. It was liberating in a way to be able to think about the possibilities of philanthropy without stores or their managers or the feelings and reactions of customers. What was important was to build for the future and identify where we could make the most impact, based on my passion for various issues. I was always mindful of what would have made my father proud to have the Syms name connected to. Without passion, you can't attract people to your cause. To get anything done of any magnitude, you need to engage people right in the heart.

My passion has always been to create a more equitable society as we are challenged with what I learned are called wicked problems. These are deep and pervasive, such as the environment, food insecurity, income inequality, and women's rights.

The last of these was always the most important for me. As Hillary Clinton said, "Women's rights are human rights."

There are many ways to improve the lives of women. One is the NOW Legal Defense and Education Fund—renamed Legal Momentum—which focuses on court cases. For many years we were corporate sponsors of their work to find solutions for gender justice that would stick. We also sponsored the National Domestic Violence phone hotline, www.thehot-line.org. I was proud that the Sy Syms Foundation was able to institute that. We had it up and running before COVID exacerbated these problems, as well as child abuse. The hotline got so many calls that we didn't have enough staff to do all the intake.

Only about 2 percent of philanthropy is spent on girls and women. To me, this is a tragedy. If women feel safe, cultures are less violent. We have an epidemic of rape, shown in all the statistics. Women's right to control their bodies through birth control and abortion are under serious attack for the first time in fifty years. The quality of life for families will decline as women feel less respected in society as a whole.

I got involved with the Girl Scouts and in 2021 was honored by them. I was often asked to be honored by many organizations I have supported and done work for, but being honored is also a lot of work. You need to understand what part of the organization's budget the event supports in the coming fiscal year and be able to produce those funds from the event. I was always open to consider the challenge. The Sy Syms Foundation did good work over many years, and still does. My continued work after the Syms reorganization—especially with the Ms. Foundation for over thirty years—had helped them grow and identify other donors.

The joy of sharing in the successes of these organizations was something I didn't expect. It was nourishing and replenishing, during a time I was mourning the loss of my father and later when I was so busy with the company and relationships. One of the best was with my assistant Rick Tereo, who started as a part-time worker during college and then was promoted to assistant buyer and then buyer for Syms. We worked together for twenty-four years.

When I speak on best practices in philanthropy, I always

stress that the nonprofit world is very different from the for-profit world. You need to adjust your expectations on speed and what you can ask people to do.

All the while, doing these things and being a woman was always an opportunity to bring more women into positions of influence. Even if that wasn't our core mission, having a woman leader can make other women more comfortable. Spell broken! You can work with us. We want the same things.

Another role many women find themselves in is that of caregiver, in business and in life. For this role, there was no partnering or support.

CHAPTER 14

Taking Care

The caregiving journey will take you to places unimaginable . . . Each day has the potential to bring to the surface life-altering issues and events that offer you the opportunity to develop skills and talents you never knew you had— resourcefulness, stamina, flexibility and faith to name a few. You won't come away from the caregiving experience the same as when you started, nor will you look at life and death in the way you did before.
—Joy Loverde, *The Complete Eldercare Planner*

Coming out of a home where I was the female oldest child, with Mom pregnant every two years, I learned through osmosis about caregiving and the need to pitch in.

After her third pregnancy, Mom suffered postpartum depression, which kept her in bed most of the time. My grandmother was living with us and caring for my mom. But a lot of responsibility fell on me, especially caring for the baby, who slept next to my bed in a crib.

During that time, my mom's mom was a diabetic. Her treatment was daily injections of insulin, with a very thick and long needle. She was four-foot-eight and weighed about eighty pounds. I remember watching her give her-self her injection in the morning. Years later I was some-times asked to give her the injection. I was always afraid I was hurting her, but she needed the insulin to live. One of the first lessons for caregiving is you can't always make your loved one happy, but you can always try to make them comfortable.

Oftentimes as a caregiver, you are helpless to actually im-prove the medical outcome. In these cases, the most impor-tant thing is to show empathy. I learned and relearned that lesson as my mother had more pregnancies and another bout of postpartum depression.

It's important, and generally overlooked, that a key role of the caregiver is to take care of themselves as well as their loved one. I consider the most challenging part of the experience is to remember to take care of yourself.

As a caregiver, your most important skill is organization. You need to organize the schedules for medicine administra-tion, with the schedule printed and visible for the times and quantities of medicine to be taken. You need an easily acces-sible list of all doctors, their contact information, and their specialties. Perhaps the most important thing in being orga-nized is to have all the insurance information for the person you're caring for and to keep the information up to date. If you're at the stage where there's a need to have additional support staff for caring for your loved one, that requires a whole new layer of organization and administration.

If there is a hospital stay, the vigilance and intervention go into hyperdrive. The bureaucracy of hospitals tends to get snarlier, and you as caregiver become the main advocate for your loved one. This means not just rubber-stamping doc-tors' decisions, but doing research, seeking new information, and second or third opinions. Arm yourself with common sense and a well-charged phone for internet research.

Caregiving can be an extra full-time job on top of whatever full-time job a woman already has. There are deliveries, pickups, appointments, and maybe squeezing in a little time for yourself. If it all gets too much, look for professional services that can pick up some of the slack.

With all this activity, it's often easy to overlook the emotional health of your loved one. It's vital to try to make sure that their joy in life be maintained and flourishes. When we're sick, we tend to be isolated, but it's much better to be part of a community as much as possible for as long as possible. Even if the community meets only once a week to make pottery, play bingo, talk current events, or fingerpaint, it can be a lifeline to someone who has been housebound.

My younger sister, Laura, was diagnosed as schizophrenic at age seventeen.

I was very close to her and was her main support for the last twenty years of her life. Although she was able to enjoy much of the years in her forties, she did relapse and needed full-time attention to administer medication that was essential for her to maintain stability and a life that was engaged with her surroundings and not succumb to the voices she heard, which was a part of the illness.

During the last twenty years of Laura's life, after much research, I realized that our culture provided very few communities for single adults. As a family we therefore became a supporter of a project in Florida through the Jewish Federation, a home for adults like my sister, who might be unable to live on their own independently.

I'm glad to say that, because of the demand, this grew and today has about thirty residents. Fortunately and intentionally, this home was close to a Syms store and Laura was able to work in it. Her job gave her life structure, meaning, and a community outside the home, and it gave us something to talk about almost every day. For twelve years she worked in the back room, checking in merchandise, but her favorite job was working in the fitting room, where she could use her terrific fashion sense and sense of style and color in commenting on what people were trying on. She was well liked and had her birthday celebrated in the store lunchroom with balloons and usually a paid "Happy Birthday" singer. All her coworkers would sing along.

One year we had a guy in a gorilla costume who entertained educators in the lunchroom during breaks for the entire day. To Laura's delight, several photos of this event were shared in *The Educator* newsletter, which came out monthly and was left in all the stores for everyone to read.

Sometimes being ill or not being in the mainstream subjects the affected person to stereotyping and antiquated attitudes toward dating or romantic relationships, or certain types of friendships. These attitudes can persuade people to remain celibate or isolated for no good reason. I was delighted to see Laura find a nice young man in her community with whom she could have a romantic relationship. It wasn't traditional, but they had a regular date night when a car would pick them up and take them to dinner and a movie. It was lovely. They would hold hands, giggle, and share experiences; they felt alive and appreciated. That sort of feeling is very important for strength and important for withstanding the indignities of illness, of which there are many.

My brother Robert suffered a crippling heart attack, his second, at age sixty-two, but managed to survive. He always enjoyed women's company, was charming, and a great storyteller. I was fortunate to find two uniquely qualified women in hospice care who gave my brother the professional attention and kindness he needed.

When he unexpectedly recovered and moved out of hospice care, to live another three years, they came home with him and continued to provide the daily support that his level of infirmity required. During my frequent visits and conversations with the two caregivers, I was constantly aware of their devotion to my brother's well-being and state of mind. I'm sure the women, who were from Jamaica and Ecuador, enriched and prolonged his life.

Even though he needed to use a wheelchair, they'd joke about going dancing and taking exotic vacations. He was quite ill this whole time, but never lost his humanity, because of how much he felt appreciated. I made sure to involve him in every decision about his health and care. Dignity and respect need to be maintained even in the toughest of situations.

The medical profession, and my experience with it, has changed over the years as small private practitioners have been rolled up into huge medical systems, leading to more bureaucracy and longer and longer disclaimers. There's a similarity in my experience to being a good entrepreneur. A good caregiver listens to her gut, just like a successful entrepreneur. When you hire somebody for your start-up and you get a funny feeling they're not getting it, or this shouldn't take this long, or there are too many slow updates, you need to act. The same goes for caregiving situations.

The most difficulty I had as a caregiver, whether as a little girl caring for my infant brother, or as a grown woman caring for the same brother, was a feeling of helplessness. It's depleting, frustrating, and ultimately an unsustainable place to be. It is to be avoided at all costs.

Most of us will not be asked to be caregivers of siblings, but more and more, with our longer lifespans, adult children are being asked to care for their parents for five, ten, even twenty-plus years.

The first responsibility I have learned in this position, is to carefully assess the financial implications of your parent living to a ripe old age of say, eighty-five-plus. The new analysis of old age says the following: sixty-five is the new "young"

old, seventy-five is the "middle-age" old, and eighty-five is
"old" old. There are more and more people living well into
their nineties, who require much more financial support than
they required when they were "young" old. Over the past few
years, the fastest growing area in real estate investment has
been the construction of assisted living communities. Whereas much of this development began in warm-weather states
like Florida, Arizona, and Nevada, today, because parents
and children want to live closer to each other in their final
years together, such developments are quickly springing up
in New York, northern California, Chicago, and other colder
climes. The benefit of this trend is your ability to be fully engaged with your parent as they may be losing some of their
vitality and mental agility.

My mom was a snowbird. For more than thirty-five years
she lived in Florida for eight months and New Jersey for
four. She was unwilling to leave the warmer climate and even
today, in her mid-nineties, is uncomfortable in temperatures
below sixty-five degrees. My mom has had a broken hip and
hip replacement, a fractured arm, macular degeneration, di-
verticulosis, and cognitive decline, just in the last five years.
Even though it was difficult to visit and review the benefits of
assisted living, it made all the difference to me that she was
in an efficient and well-run assisted living community.

Don't think that once your loved one is in an assisted living community, your caregiving journey is over. It does help
if the assisted living community has on-site medical staff. In
order to find this for my mom, we decided she should move,
in the first year of COVID, from a community that had no
medical care, to one that did. Assessing the pros and cons of
each choice may be required at different times during the
"old" old years.

During this journey, you need to take care of yourself. You
can't know how long the journey will be and what turns it

will take. You need to be prepared with the right information and stay healthy.

Perhaps the most emotionally charged caregiving situation I have experienced was the one with my dad. Always trying to be respectful of one another's privacy and at the same time caring and supporting one another. When I became a mother very late in life, my dad was unsure of my continued commitment to Syms the company and him in particular. He saw in the months and years after I had my son that my commitment to him and the company was very much the same. There was time to be a mother and CEO.

I have a pillow embroidered with the motto: *If you don't think you can buy happiness, you haven't been shopping in the right place.* So let's talk about dressing properly. Dressing women was my career for four decades, so I'd like to offer a tip or two.

CHAPTER 15

Clothes Make the First Impression

Men their rights and nothing more; women their rights and nothing less.
—Susan B. Anthony

First impressions are critical, and the first thing we see is clothing.

Using my experience as a purveyor and consumer of women's clothing, as well as my education at Fashion Institute of Technology and elsewhere, I gave speeches to several groups at the end of the 1980s on these topics, as well as contributing to a chapter in a book called *Real Life 101* by Susan Kleinman. This chapter is an updated distillation of those thoughts.

> I've always been a proponent of clothes that somehow make me stand out. The only time you want to fade into the woodwork is when you're afraid of getting fired. Otherwise, you want to stand out . . . to be recognized. Looking put-together or intentional is an important part of self-confidence.

The negative impressions people get as a result of what you are wearing are very subtle. Your boss won't consciously realize that she doesn't trust you because your seams are puckered; she'll just notice a vague feeling in the pit of her stomach that tells her you haven't impressed her.

To dress well, you've got to know how to shop well. These days, many time-strapped women shop online. In fact, some don't even buy—they rent. Websites including Rent the Runway, Armoire, and Stitch Fix let you get advice online from a stylist, get a selection of clothes sent to you, and charge a small fee. You can wear and send them all back or buy them if you wish. These are all top-designer clothes.

The most important thing to bring to any shopping trip—including virtual ones—is your sense of value and your sense of brand. You need a sense of value to recognize quality and styling at a low price. You have to know what brands look good on you. Order a bunch of dresses and try them on!

What's made well? Once you have an idea of that, you can look for the best price. Then you can find bargains, which are good quality clothes that last three to five years and might look like they cost more than they did.

If you are someone who has no time to shop, or if you dislike shopping, you probably want to buy the best quality possible without shopping around for the best bargain. If you wear certain clothes a lot, you'll probably want them to have better quality than if you only wear an outfit once or twice a year. If you like to keep up with fashion and change your wardrobe frequently, you may be happier buying less expensive clothing that will work well for only one season.

You don't need to spend a fortune to put together a basic wardrobe, if you shop smart. Quality in clothes depends on fabric and craftsmanship. The more you know about different types of fibers and how to tell whether a garment is well made, the easier it is to tell good quality.

It doesn't do you much good to buy the best quality piece of clothing you can afford if it doesn't flatter you or make you feel comfortable, so fit and knowing what looks good on you are important. Knowing where to shop, how to plan your wardrobe, and how to take care of your clothes are also part of being a good consumer.

What you pick depends on your pocketbook and the lifestyle you lead. While price is often an indication of quality, it isn't always, and there are ways to be a smart consumer and get good quality whether you buy couture fashion, designer clothes, or off-the-rack merchandise. Quality in clothes is determined by the fabric and the craftsmanship that goes into making them.

By examining the labels on a piece of clothing, you can tell what it's made of and how you should clean it. By knowing something about the fibers, you'll have some idea how long it will last and how it will perform. For example, clothes made of natural fibers—wool, cotton, linen, and silk—are usually of better quality and last longer than clothes made of synthetic fibers. However, they are also more expensive and require more upkeep. You can't just throw a silk blouse into a washing machine and expect it to come out looking good.

But, if you buy good silk, you can hand-wash it, using a product such as Woolite in lukewarm water. If there's a stain, you do have to send it to the cleaners. Silk obviously takes more time and money to care for than synthetics. On the other hand, if you travel a lot, you'll appreciate the easy-care aspect of many synthetic fabrics. It's often hard to tell the difference between a good polyester blouse and a silk one just by looking.

Your choice between natural and synthetics depends on cost, degree of quality you want, and the time and money you want to spend for upkeep. By reading labels and knowing something about fibers, you'll know what to expect from a garment before you buy it.

Think of a Cadillac or a Rolex watch. Those brands stand for a certain level of quality. The whole history of the company goes along with the brand name.

As a consumer, you're protected by having a genuinely identified brand item. The company has a reputation and a history. It's quite different from buying something that has a private label or a dummied-up label, which is a label that's simply a name without a history as to its quality.

For that kind of clothing, you don't know where to go if the seams start coming apart, you don't know who to write to. No one is standing behind the name. It doesn't exist. A brand name is a consumer protection because there's responsibility and accountability.

Brand names carry with them a certain level of craftsmanship. Craftsmanship refers to the way clothes are made. No matter what the brand name, and especially if it's a brand you're not familiar with, check the way the clothes are made. Look at the collars and lapels, making sure they stand up, roll, or lie exactly as the designer intended them to. Look at the seams. Are they going to unravel or split with wear? Does the pattern match up at the seams?

Good quality skirts are lined, and the best skirts have a separate lining that is attached to the inside. Check zippers and fasteners, making sure there aren't any puckers. Buttons can always be replaced, but buttonholes should be smoothly finished. With coats or jackets, check the quality of the lining and look for a back pleat so that the lining won't tear at the armholes.

While you should pay attention to the way clothes are made and the fabric, buying good-quality clothes doesn't do much good if they don't fit right. Fit is very individual. Some people like to wear tight clothing. They like to feel the fabric pulling across their shoulder blades. Now that would not be considered a good fit, but if that's the way you like to wear clothing and the way you feel comfortable, go right ahead.

Ideally, for the wear of the garment and for the most complimentary look to your body, a good fit should skim your body lines. It should not have stress points in the fabric, because that means it's a little small in that area. Nor should it be gaping or puckering, because that indicates that it's a little too big, or there is too much fabric for the length of your body. Sometimes you need to shop around to find those designers and brand names that fit your body type.

Generally speaking, if you want to purchase something that needs to have major seams tampered with, it's probably not a good fit, so don't buy it. One exception is a man's suit jacket, where letting out the middle back seam of the jacket is not considered a major alteration. Usually the only alterations you should have are those that don't change the flow of the fabric, like the length, including the length of the sleeves and legs. You don't want to disrupt the look.

I would pass on reconstructing the shoulders and other major alterations.

Every fashion magazine, website, TikTok influencer, and high-priced personal shopper gives tips on how to plan and build a basic wardrobe. It's very individual and it depends on your lifestyle. Clothes should last three to five years with normal wear. Adding a few items every year tends to freshen things up. It helps to be disciplined when reviewing your wardrobe. If you don't "love" it or haven't worn it for a year or more, consider getting rid of it. I used to keep everything, and that meant nothing ever looked new because I'd be taking something that was too old and placing it with something that was this year's. Sometimes that can be charming, but more often than not, you just spoil the new thing.

Over the years, I've become much more disciplined to say, Yes, I did love it three years ago; it's not going to kill me to let it go. And I give my clothes to charity, to people who can really use them. It feels good, it makes sense, I usually don't miss them, and it leaves room to buy new things.

All of us have limited closet space and that brings up the next point: taking care of your clothes. Once you've spent a fair amount of money on your wardrobe, it pays to take care of it. If you have an entire closet of polyester, you don't have to be too concerned with taking care of clothes, but most of us have a combination of blends and natural fibers. In that case, we want to make sure there's space between your clothes in your closet. You should allow some air to go between the garments.

Don't leave garments on wire hangers. There are those wonderful hangers that have padding on them, the quilted ones, and there are less expensive ones in wood and plastic. This type of hanger makes it almost impossible to pack your clothes too close together. So take your clothes off the wire hangers you get from the dry cleaner's and take them out of those plastic bags. The plastic doesn't let the garment breathe.

You also don't want to have a closet that has a radiator in it or that is near an open window. You don't want your clothes exposed to fluctuations in temperature. When you get a stain on a piece of clothing, you'll want to treat it as soon as possible.

How you should treat it depends on the type of stain and the type of fabric.

For example, bloodstains on washable fabrics should be soaked in cold water first, whereas grass stains on the same kind of fabric should be pretreated with a detergent and then washed with hot water. You can get information on how to treat various kinds of stains from government websites and from publications put out by the International Fabricare Institute. Sometimes you're best off by taking the garment to a dry cleaner. If you have to dry-clean something after every wear, you might just as well not buy it. Dry-cleaning destroys fiber.

What's recommended for a wool suit, for example, is to dry-clean only after it's been worn six or seven times. The rest of the time, let it hang in your bathroom with the steam going, or just beat it out with a brush. Your clothing lasts longer the less frequently you dry-clean it.

The Federal Trade Commission puts out information on-line on care labels. You can also get information from magazines and books, as well as online from manufacturers and from government agencies on a number of consumer-related subjects. It's all there for us and it's just a matter of taking the time and making the commitment to understand what we're purchasing. It takes a little patience, but it's well worth the investment because you can expect longer and better wear when it comes to clothes and a sense of feeling good and spending your money wisely when it comes to any consumer purchase.

I think you must know what looks good on you, and what makes you feel like you look good. You need a certain amount of knowledge, which you get from experience, from reading magazines, and from talking to other people, about various brand names—designer names and manufacturers' labels—so you'll know what you can expect.

Now that we've got the dressing basics down, let's look at another of my passions, helping family businesses thrive.

CHAPTER 16

Starting a Business, Family or Not

We're just sweeping dirty dishes under the rug.
—Archie Bunker

When I came into Syms, I started studying the dynamics of family businesses. I read every article on the topic, talked to every expert I could find, contacted every association that dealt with family businesses, and surveyed people in successful family businesses to see how they handled the unusual pressures and opportunities that arise when you mix family and business. In the end, I became an expert and wrote a book on the topic. But those were side benefits; my primary objective was to learn, so I could manage and perform better.

According to several researchers, family firms employ half of the nation's workforce. Many people think of family businesses as the mom-and-pop corner drugstore or deli, but the reality is quite different. Just ask Lee Iacocca. He found out the hard way that Ford was still very much controlled by the Ford family.

Ivan Lansberg, a professor at the Yale School of Organization and Management, found that seventy-five of the *Fortune* 500 firms are controlled by families, including companies such as Ford and DuPont. Of course, classifying companies as to whether they're a family-controlled businesses or not, depends on how one defines a family business. To Professor Lansberg, the critical factor is whether the family has input and influence in the management process.

In some family-controlled businesses, the family owns 100 percent of the business. Estée Lauder is one of those. In others, the family's stake may not be quite as high, but the family still influences the decisions and policy. Family businesses cover the entire gamut of industries, from modeling and the famous Ford Modeling Agency, to real estate with a company like Olympia & York, which was owned by the Reichmann brothers of Toronto, and was the largest owner of New York City commercial real estate.

Family businesses come in all sizes, but they all started small. In some cases, they've made their owners very rich. The Walton family controls the Walmart retail empire founded by Sam Walton. Its market capitalization is north of $240 billion. Mars, Incorporated, which manufactures Snickers, M&M's, and Milky Way, along with pet food, rice, and electronics, has made its owners, the Mars family, into one of the richest in America with a net worth of $94 billion dollars, according to *Business Insider*.

Some industries are particularly known for family businesses, such as publishing, where names like the Sulzbergers of the *New York Times*, the Grahams and Meyers of the *Washington Post*, and the Hearsts of the Hearst Corporation, instantly come to mind. The Binghams of Kentucky, whose press empire collapsed because of family disputes, played out a drama as tragic as any of Shakespeare's.

Family businesses exist in fiction as well as fact. Family businesses are interesting, intriguing, and the source for countless novels, movies, and television series. I don't know whether you'd consider the Mafia a family business, but Mario Puzo obviously did in his novels, including *The Godfather.*

Family businesses account for 80 to 90 percent of all the nation's businesses, large and small, and they contribute between 40 and 60 percent of our gross national product. I believe the family business is an attractive, viable option that shouldn't be overlooked when you're considering a career or career change.

Before you decide to go into a family business, you should consider a number of things, especially if you want to be successful in it. The most important things to think about are your attitudes, the skills you have to bring, and your relationships with the other family members who are already in the business.

Let's begin with the relationship. There are as many kinds of relationships as there are types of relatives. A family business isn't always the father bringing in the child. It's often a wife or husband bringing in a spouse or an entrepreneur bringing in an uncle, brother, or cousin. Each relationship has its own separate dynamics and its own unique emotional baggage, depending on past history.

The relationship I know best is a father-daughter one, but I think that generally, if you are to succeed, you have to have a certain amount of respect for the family member who runs the business. It's essential to get along with him or her. I know offspring of entrepreneurs who assume it's their right to enter their parent's business simply because it's there and it's easy to get hired. That's probably a mistake.

If you don't have a family business you want to join, start one of your own.

More and more women are starting their own companies,

and I'm convinced a major driver of that is the shameful treatment women CEOs have received over the years.

Even today, women are often brought into a failing situation as CEO when nobody else wants the job. Why? Because we are so few. Why are there so many women in middle management, but you rarely see them higher up? It's not a lack of talent. A lot of them realize they are being given the top job in order to fail, so they opt out.

Many middle managers are saying they might as well start their own company. If I'm going to fail, I'll fail on my own terms.

I'm convinced this is a major impetus for female entrepreneurship, as was the COVID shutdown of 2020. Stuck at home with the kids and often part-time teaching duties, many young and not-so-young women decided to virtually launch the jewelry or cooking or fashion advice business they had dreamed about. Some failed, but many succeeded, and the flame of entrepreneurship burned bright.

Expectations for women make it so much harder to succeed. Girls are doing better in school, but that doesn't mean opportunities should be taken away from them. Our culture needs adjustment so roles are healthier for both boys and girls. Fairer expectations will make society healthier.

The starting point for becoming an entrepreneur is to look at yourself and take charge. You need to tell yourself often, "I am an entrepreneur," because there are plenty of people who will tell you otherwise.

In my case, they said that my position as CEO of Syms came because I was the founder's daughter. Nonsense. As I worked up through the company, I took ownership of the projects I was involved in. I felt passionate about them. The fact that my name was on the building meant a lot to me. I never said, "It's not my job." If something needed to be done, I got it done.

Your accomplishments are yours—not your father's, your

husband's, your boss's, or your teacher's. They are *yours*. A tidal wave of entrepreneurial activity is sweeping in and it's being led by women. *Fortune* magazine estimates that 70 percent of the new businesses founded in the US each year are owned by women. Women are founding companies at over twice the rate men are.

It is no coincidence that in the *Peanuts* cartoons, it was Lucy who set up a booth to sell advice. She's the entrepreneur in that group. I hope that none of you are saying to yourself, "I'm an employee, so this has no relevance to me."

Thinking like an entrepreneur is a survival skill for employees as well as for the self-employed. No matter what company you are in, you will be asked to be—and you will want to be—a profit center. Your piece of business needs to be connected to the bottom line in a positive way. When you go for a job, inside or outside of the company, you'll want to be able to express your value in terms of your entrepreneurial performance.

Whether you're in a company or out on your own, you have to find a niche—an area where you can offer value. One of my favorite stories is about a couple that had a small, successful store. Then a humongous store opened up on one side of them with a tremendous sign that said, *The World's Lowest Prices*, and an even bigger store opened up on the other side of them with a sign that said, *The Biggest Selection in the Universe*. The husband went to a lawyer to see about lawsuits, but the wife got out the paint and a board and made a sign to go over their door. The sign said, *Main Entrance*.

The essence of being an entrepreneur is taking charge. According to qualitative research done by Lee Hecht Harrison, the number one reason why women become entrepreneurs is the need to be in control of their lives and confident of their own abilities. Women become entrepreneurs so they can create their own fate. Realistically, you can't rely on a corporation to provide lifetime employment. In the last decades, even companies like AT&T and IBM—which used to hold out the promise of lifetime employment—have cut jobs.

While big companies are changing, in many instances, their old boy networks remain fairly robust. You might get stuck in a "pink ghetto," an area where the pay is low because the work has traditionally been done by females, and you are likely to run into a glass ceiling, which somehow stops women from making it into the very top floor where the top executives sit.

According to a 2023 Russell Reynolds study, men constitute 53 percent of the US workforce, but hold 72 percent of the positions of vice presidents or above. That means the 47 percent of women in the workforce hold just 28 percent of the top jobs.

Women hold 45 percent of the middle management jobs like assistant vice president and office manager, but only 5 percent of the higher positions. What happens when all those women middle managers hit the glass ceiling? Many are moving out and becoming entrepreneurs—and because of their middle management experience, they have a better chance of success.

There's no rule that says you'll spend your career either in a company or as an entrepreneur. More and more people are crossing back and forth between the two types of employment. You might start a company as an entrepreneur and then get bought out. Or you may start as an employee and decide you could do the job better on your own.

When the National Federation of Independent Business asked 3000 start-up business owners where they got the idea for their new enterprise, 74 percent said "from my previous employment."

As an entrepreneur, you need to be nimble and ready to seize opportunities when you see them. We are facing a world that is changing more rapidly than ever before. Jobs will disappear, companies will be reorganized. The average worker will change jobs every three years and will change careers three times.

When things are changing that fast, the only viable response to the inevitability of change is to stay flexible, so you can nimbly move from one role to another. This calls for continuous learning.

One area where the need for continuous learning has been particularly clear is the field of computers. It's impossible to underestimate the role of computers in making entrepreneurship both necessary and possible. The bad news is that computers are replacing lots of middle managers; the good news is that computers and high-tech systems are creating new opportunities and helping entrepreneurs compete with larger businesses. Today we also have to consider artificial intelligence, or AI, which by all indications is going to transform how we use computers. Or how computers use us. Many first drafts of company documents and materials today are AI influenced. From information fed in, AI programs spit back out a written template, allowing people working together to start with a shared version.

Being an early adapter of offerings from Google and others for AI enhancements is a great risk. But it is a risk that can have huge payoffs for consultants, for marketing, and for management. At this point, we don't understand how this all will be incorporated and meshed with human skills in these areas that are necessary to be successful. It appears at this time that AI will be raising the bar on not only what we as individuals know, but also on the simultaneous access to information we want to have that we don't presently even know we don't have. If that isn't confusing enough, there seems to be no consensus about how to measure AI's added value, if any.

These are things that any entrepreneur needs to be aware of and on top of. If it sounds like a lot of work, it is. I'll make the case that women have a greater chance of advancement in entrepreneurial settings than they do in corporate ones. But I won't claim that it's easy.

An entrepreneur needs to know how to motivate herself. You have to believe in your mission. Successful entrepreneurs often don't sell, they testify, and the power of their belief makes the sale. Do whatever you can to stay positive. When you find a story that moves you, cut it out, put it on the refrigerator, and reread it every time you need that extra push.

Take your work personally. If you find your entrepreneurial energy giving out, remember that your name is associated with everything you do. That's often enough to get you going.

If that doesn't work, set up a system of rewards for yourself. Just remember, as an entrepreneur, you're the captain—you carry the ball. So, you have to keep your spirits up, your goals clear, and your attention focused.

A lot of people make the mistake of thinking that being an entrepreneur means being a solo player. Actually, entrepreneurship is the ultimate team sport, and the entrepreneur is the leader of the team.

The first quality a leader needs is enthusiasm. Every time I talk to an outstanding leader, I find myself thinking, "Wow. I want to work with them." They radiate excitement about their work. It's contagious, so they get more out of their employees, more out of their suppliers, and more out of people who are just friends of the company.

I used to think that you could mold and discipline people so they would work harder. I'm not so sure anymore. But I am sure that you can provide leadership for them and create an environment where they will thrive. Entrepreneurs are leaders. If you're willing to lead, it's amazing how many people will be ready to follow.

How do you learn to do all this? The first rule is to trust yourself.

One of the bestselling books ever written in America is *Dr. Spock's Baby and Child Care*. A big reason for the book's phenomenal success is the message in its first line, which reads, *You know more than you think you do.* That's also one of my points about thinking like an entrepreneur.

> You can rely on your instincts. Trust that voice inside of your head; it will give you good guidance. If something feels wrong, it probably is. If someone makes you nervous, watch out for them. If something seems too easy, there's probably a catch. You are going to be asking other people to treat you as an expert and trust you; start by setting an example and trusting yourself.

An essential part of trusting yourself is living your values. This may sound corny, but the classic virtues that scholars have written about will serve as your guideposts. They are how you know whether a decision is a good one. I have found that good, ethical decisions pay off in the long run.

Living your values is an area where many women may have an advantage, or at least, more practice. Men have, as a rule, been better at compartmentalizing their lives. A guy could go to work and be a complete savage, then come home and be a wonderful dad. Fewer women have been able to do that, and that's actually a good thing.

Today the 24/7 media makes sure that all leaders have, effectively, no private lives. Even if you're great at compartmentalizing, people will know what you're really like. If you're a phony, they won't follow you.

In corporate settings, it's important to manage relationships with people you work for. An entrepreneur manages in all directions. In my case, it was important for me to know how to manage the relationship with my father, but the same would apply to any boss. Be attentive over time to what your bosses respond to. I knew, for example, that my father hated the word *problem*. If I went in and said, "I have a problem," I lost him—he wouldn't hear the rest of what I had to say. So instead I said, "There is a situation," or "It has come to my attention that . . ."

Be careful about timing. I knew that just after my father played tennis was the best time to bring something up to him— particularly if he won!

> Understand the boss's attention span. A good technique is to stop talking for a moment and see if the other person can come back at you with a good question. It takes self-confidence to do this, but it's a great test. If the listener realizes that you're still in the middle of things, you're fine. If he or she thinks you're through, you are through, and may have been through for a while.

As soon as you can, start to give something back to the communities that made it possible for you to be a success. Again, the popular image of the entrepreneur is wrong. Entrepreneurs, for the most part, aren't people who hoard their wealth. They're generally involved with their communities and very generous.

It's important to find ways to help that are comfortable for you to affirm your values; and it's important to realize that you can give more than just money.

If you are a successful entrepreneur, you can be a role model, or even a mentor for young people. Being an entrepreneur is hard work, but thinking like an entrepreneur is relatively straightforward.

I firmly believe that more women starting more businesses

will both benefit and change our country in ways we may not even anticipate. Countries like Iceland and New Zealand show how equal numbers of women in business translates to more women in public service.

And importantly, it will help fill the pipeline for those coveted corporate board seats.

CHAPTER 17

Being on a Board

*If you're a woman who wants to join a board, learn to
play golf.*
—Anonymous

That old joke sadly contains a big kernel of truth. Boards of directors of both for-profit and not-for-profit organizations are still too often these days made up of the CEOs' contacts from the country club, college, other boards, or from within the company. While women have begun to break into this pipeline and on to boards, we still have a long way to go.

According to a 2023 Deloitte study, women globally hold 23.3 percent of board seats and were 6 percent of CEOs. While that percentage has grown steadily over the years, Deloitte estimates that at that rate of growth, women would reach parity with men on boards in 2038 at the earliest!

That's unacceptable. While this is personal to me, I believe it would benefit business and philanthropy to have more women's voices and perspectives in the rooms where the decisions are made.

By sharing my own experiences, I hope to encourage more women to do what it takes to get on a board, any board, and make your voices heard while you are there. We've got to grow the pipelines of associations, networks, and social media profiles so that these women are noticed. It can no longer just be golf.

For women seeking board opportunities, relationships are the places to start. Even today, only a very small percentage of board seats are filled through recruiters, though it doesn't hurt to get your name and résumé in front of some recruiters too.

Getting an invitation to join a board is a function of putting yourself out there through meetings, speeches, volunteering, social media, and whatever else you can think of. It's also a matter of luck and timing.

As with most job searches, boards are looking for people with relevant experience, so it's hard to get that first invitation. But if you've run anything from a Girl Scout troop, to a PTA chapter, to a nonprofit, to a private or public company, you have credentials worth utilizing.

To get started, look for a nonprofit in your area that tickles one of your interests, or exploits one of your talents. Since most of nonprofit boards are uncompensated, they often welcome volunteers who bring an interest or experience to the table. Among many examples are homeless shelters, food banks, and animal welfare societies (and yes, the Girl Scouts and the PTA.)

It's harder to get on a paid corporate board. For that, you need a track record running something, an in-demand skill, connections, or talent that will enhance the existing composition of the board. Compensated positions also require vetting of your resume and references, often by outside agencies.

If you're interested in a particular company, read everything you can about them, especially their annual reports. These all contain biographies of directors and the dates their terms expire, as well as information on when they might be retiring. Look for areas of expertise that you have that the board members don't. You still need a connection or way in, as well as luck, to get that invitation.

I always tell women seeking board work that family-owned, for-profit private companies that are often the best places to start.

My first experience on a board was, of course, at Syms, as an executive serving as an inside director. Our board usually had six members: Sy, me, our chief financial officer from the inside, an outside independent director who was typically a former retail executive—from, for example, Bloomingdale's—an account or vendor, and an investment banker.

We functioned with six, but really could have used eight, especially after the adoption of the Sarbanes-Oxley Act of 2002 which vastly increased the amount of records and information we had to produce and keep.

My first outside directorship was with Midlantic Bank, a medium-sized bank holding company that had taken over Philadelphia-based Continental Bancorp in 1987. While I was a board member, Midlantic was taken over by the much-bigger PNC financial services group. This was during what shrewd observers called the Pac-Man era, with bigger fish swallowing smaller ones, especially in the area of regional financial businesses.

Mergers can be crucial for the companies on whose boards you serve. They affect all the stakeholders, from management, to employees, to shareholders, to customers. Good ones create more choices for customers. Bad ones, as we saw in the case of Syms and Filene's Basement, can doom the whole enterprise.

The Midlantic merger was pretty cut-and-dried. It was a great fit and great for shareholders, including several of my fellow directors. As a principle, I never bought shares in the companies whose boards I sat on, unless it was part of the compensation. At one point I had to buy shares of Syms in order to file ownership of more than 50 percent control, but all of those purchases were public and documented.

I was always aware when I was the only woman on a board,

and the CEO of a public company that prided itself on respect and ethical dealing with all of our stakeholders, to avoid even a hint of self-dealing or conflict of interest. I felt this strongly as both a woman and my father's daughter.

Having a moral compass was both a blessing and a curse. I felt the added pressure of being the very public spokesperson for Syms. And I had a very narrow space within which to operate ethically. I remember remarking on how many directors benefited directly from the PNC acquisition of Midlantic. It was all legal and the merger did create value, but I just didn't want anything to do with that.

I was privileged to serve on the board of Rite Aid, based in Philadelphia and the third-biggest pharmacy chain in the country, for more than fourteen years. I was introduced to the company by a friend, and I had already developed a good impression of its well-run stores because I shopped in them often.

The first interview with their recruiter in my office didn't go well. I had told my assistant to hold all my calls. With no phones ringing, it seemed to him that I didn't do much and wasn't really connected or in demand.

Fortunately, I got a second chance. Their CEO flew inro the small airport at Teterboro, New Jersey, near our distribution center and came to my office. This time I told my assistant to make sure the phone rang every ten minutes. I gave him a tour and my spiel about Syms and was invited to join the board.

I was a Rite Aid director through four CEOs and two failed merger attempts. Both times the FTC vetoed the mergers, saying the resulting company would be anticompetitive.

By the end of my tenure, it was clear that a giant elephant named Amazon had entered the room and the pharmacy business would never be the same. It was clear even in 2016 that pharmacies needed to be either part of a giant national chain or a small, boutique operation serving a select slice of a local market. Being somewhere in the middle, as was Rite Aid, didn't cut it anymore.

Some of my most uncomfortable moments as an outside board member have concerned the effectiveness and performance of the CEO. One experience that stands out to me occurred when I was a board member of a for-profit organization, where the board and management had been working on a merger that would likely save the company.

The merger failed because of many issues, not the least of which was the business environment, along with press coverage that was mischaracterized at first but later corrected. But as a result of the erroneous articles, shareholders were split fifty-fifty on whether the merger was a good idea.

Voices within and without the company were calling for the firing of the CEO. I wasn't in favor of this. As a board member evaluating all the information known to us, I felt the CEO should remain, but in the presence of equally sincere opposition, I suggested we form a committee to study the matter and report to the full board. This is a standard way of getting work that usually isn't handled by the complete board presented in a digestible fashion, often by calling on outside expertise.

On the committee were board members both for and against the continued employment of the CEO. It was our job to thoroughly and fairly investigate our options. That work consumed the committee for months. This was a process and not a knee-jerk reaction.

All of this took time. It was incumbent upon the board to assure management that there would be a deliberation calendar that responded to the urgency of getting this decision made. Even with that urgency, it took close to three months before a decision by the committee went to the full board, with reasons for why it was the correct decision at this time to maintain the employment of the CEO.

We also were able to establish adjusted metrics for evaluating the CEO's performance that were different from how he had been evaluated prior to the failed merger. The full board was satisfied with this, and eventually so was the investment community. I remain convinced it was the right decision.

While we were split, our meetings were always muted and fact-based. Everyone was exhausted by the months and months of discussions. I figured we made about 11 cents an hour during this intense time of service.

A director doesn't just sit in meetings, although you definitely sit in a lot of meetings. What's important is ideas, and the best ideas a director can bring are those management hadn't thought of or thought of and rejected for the wrong reasons. A great board member also has the strength of character, experience, and insight to pull away from board consensus.

I had the opportunity to be an advisor to the board of a very successful small manufacturing company that was preparing for the third generation of the family to come into the business. The competitive market for their highly technical product had changed and much of the manufacturing of it had gone overseas.

The family and the board had to evaluate how much investment was needed and how big a risk it would be to move their production overseas to remain competitive, or to find a way to somehow reposition their product as a high-quality alternative and therefore create a special niche.

Doing that would require heavy expenses as the transition was taking place and perhaps even losing the legacy of the good name of the company. When all of these issues were reviewed by the family and board, it was determined that the third generation might be better served by selling the company. There was no way to know in advance if this was the right decision, or whether a third-generation family member would turn out to have been a transformational leader. You only have the best information you can glean at the time.

Timing is everything, because even though the board made this recommendation, the family dragged its feet and didn't seriously consider the board's advice until a couple of years later, when the value of the company had diminished.

Once I was one of two women on a not-for-profit board. The other woman was someone who had a lot of money and made a significant monetary contribution to the success of the organization. But the price was high because she was extremely disruptive. She always asked questions or made comments that put the conversation back to the beginning or undermined the presenter. Something was off in her appreciation of social interaction.

Because I was a woman, the chairman of the board asked if I would try to get friendly with her and see if I could get through to her. I did and it worked, but not all the time. I was able to answer some of her questions outside the boardroom, which was helpful. But after a while it was exhausting to me personally. She eventually moved off the board.

She did maintain her financial support, though. It's vital, especially in nonprofits, never to burn a bridge. The more names you have on your home page identifying people involved with your cause, the better, even if they are now a bit less active. Keep relations cordial, even if there are disagreements.

There are almost as many different kinds of boards as there are boards. In the nonprofit sector, some may be working boards with hands-on control of decision-making or fundraising and fiduciary responsibilities, but they're always policy-reviewing boards. In the for-profit world, the CEO makes policy that is approved but usually not created by the board. Common to both is the responsibility for the financial health of the organization. Boards often oversee outside audits of the books to make sure everything is being done legally and reported in a timely and accurate way.

The idea of a board can expand in various ways. One of my favorite examples is that of my friend Elinor Guggenheimer's New York Women's Forum.

She recruited a representative from every women's organization in the state of New York, creating a humungous board that never actually met, but by dividing into committees was fairly effective at influencing legislation that was important to women and families. This was The New York Women's Agenda.

The giant board had a strong leader in Elinor and that was key. You need strong leadership to pursue initiatives. The Orpheus Chamber Orchestra famously has no leader, and while that might work for chamber music, it doesn't usually work in a bigger universe. For most purposes, you need leaders.

To find them, most organizations create search committees among directors. I've been on several. My father and I helped find the second dean of the Sy Syms School of Business. The first one had been dean of a major university business school. We thought this was really great, so that's where we looked. We didn't appreciate that taking over an entity in its midlife, with an established budget, faculty, and student body, is very different than a start-up and requires different skills. We eventually found the right person.

While I continue to be proud of the contribution my dad and I made both at Syms and through philanthropy, such as the Sy Syms School of Business, I do worry about where we've come as a nation.

We're at an inflection point as a country, which has left many of us exhausted. To close this book, I'd like to offer some reflections on how we can all recharge our batteries.

CHAPTER 18

Recharging Your Battery

*Gratitude is the secret of life. The important thing is to give
thanks for everything. Whoever has learned this knows
what it means to live.*
—Albert Schweitzer

In 2014 my husband and I decided to get a hybrid car.
We're all about preserving the species and the planet for
future generations, and we'd been following the progress of
automobiles being run on electricity with either batteries or
plug-ins. My mother had been one of the first to sign up for
a Prius. I remember being so impressed with how quiet the
drive was.

Before being able to buy what turned out to be a leased
Volvo hybrid, we had to install a new outlet in our garage.
The reason I share this experience is that I think the same
recharging needs to happen to us as we enter different phases
of our adult life that require different skills and make different demands on us.

After leaving corporate America and Syms and becoming
actively and passionately involved with the ERA Coalition
and then the start-up ERA Project in 2021, my energy was
focused on getting that off the ground. I worked with a dedicated group of board members from the coalition who had

left to establish the first-ever think tank in a nonpartisan setting. That group would be critical in providing the research and legal arguments for implementation of the ERA and the expansion of the ERA work to the states.

As I write about this experience, I have a renewed sense of exhaustion and remember how completely depleted I felt. By 2022, in the midst of the COVID lockdown, I wanted nothing more than an escape. I'm sure much of the world felt the same. Fortunately for me, I found a way to pursue this by applying to a program at Harvard called the Advanced Leadership Initiative.

I had a friend who had done it a few years earlier and had mentioned its benefits to me. The program, she said, enabled her to figure out how to use her experience and start a new phase of her life with a feeling of giving back.

One day, I picked up the phone and called the head of admissions to get the scoop. The program was for people who had at least twenty-five years of work experience, and whose lives had been more than just their job. Once accepted, the participant has the entire university at their disposal for a core curriculum and other courses that support their pursuit of the next steps in their life.

The initiative was started in 2005 by Harvard professors Rosabeth Moss Kanter, Rakesh Khurana, and Nitin Nohria at Harvard Business School. I realized how fortunate I was to be able even to consider a program like this. To be able to push the *pause* button to reboot your energies is an extraordinary chance at regeneration. The program is limited to about forty-five participants. My group ranged in ages from forty-two to seventy-eight years old, from countries from India to Costa Rica.

What a unique gift in my life's journey it was, being a member of a cohort having equal numbers of men and women, with men and women having equal authority, accomplishments, and agency. All of us came from very different backgrounds—corporate, not-for-profit, government careers. One of the participants was a professional writer. No one was a stereotype. No one was what you expected. Everyone was respectful of each other's uniqueness. For the first time in my life, this convening allowed me to see firsthand how extraordinary the outcomes can be when men and women work together as real equals. I never really felt that at Syms.

It was an environment I had always hoped for, but never found. Even if going to Harvard for ALI felt like being a kid in an intellectual candy store where nothing has calories, it over delivered on my expectations to discover gender parity as an exhilarating experience. I had always thought that the best outcomes happened when men and women work together. My cohort experience at ALI proved it.

Everyone was pursuing different projects, and we were all expected to leave after our year at Harvard with a plan. Part of the admissions process was to submit your ideas about what areas you would pursue.

My plan was to continue my work with women gaining equality under the law, so I took a shortcut on the application. I just referred the admissions committee to the two organizations I had helped start in this area.

Mike Emery, head of admissions, called me to discuss my essay. Only three paragraphs. I told him Sy had taught me that if I had something to say, I should write it on the inside of a matchbook. I had to explain that Sy, being a pipe smoker, always had a matchbook in his pocket and scribbled notes on it. While I don't smoke a pipe, I always carry a small notepad and pencil and trained myself to keep things simple and to the point. Mike chuckled. "That's not how the committee looks at things. Try to turn each paragraph into a page." I did and admired the fact that all of us, despite our station in life, had to go through the same process.

Coming out of our cohort, we had projects that focused on saving the Atlantic shoreline from pollution, translating literature to braille for blind children in India, arts education for deaf children, programs to address generational gaps in understanding of science, inner-city housing plans for the unhoused, and on and on, including ideas to address the wicked problems in our lives. And we learned the definition of a wicked problem.

The problems we tackled are so large that they impact every part of our society—universal education, health care, climate change, and we added one: the maintenance of democracy and how to keep it vibrant. This last issue wasn't on the radar before 2016. I was active in that interest group and was proud to be able to present to my group a program by Freedom House highlighting the health of democracies around the world, which was not showing a positive trend.

Now that I am a graduate, I'm pleased to see Harvard supporting the establishment of alumni groups for the 600 graduates of this program. Because we're worldwide, there's an exciting opportunity to continue to support one another on these societal issues. I'm a member of the steering committee of alumni groups in the tristate area.

Looking at this additional adult education, I see it as us needing to remain lifelong students. Although youth and its enormous creativity is important, the wisdom and perspective we have during the last quarter of our lives needs to be part of the mix in solving the wicked problems in the world. We are also at the point in our lives where many of us have the resources to put our money toward the creation of a solution even if it will take many years to accomplish.

Harvard also gave me the motivation and tools to reflect on how we can all improve our outlooks.

Be more intentional about what you say yes to and what you say no to. As you get into the eighth inning, you become more aware of your mortality. Any projects that might take you ten years to finish may not be such a good idea. Break them down into smaller chunks. Know how you can advise the folks in their third and fourth innings to take the lead.

When you look at the time you have, time becomes much more precious.

There's a Chinese proverb: "Time is worth its weight in gold. But you can buy gold and time can't be purchased."

When you see rays of sunshine, you need to stop and be grateful and say thanks, so you're fortified for the next thicket when things don't go right.

People always need to be listened to and see others leading by example. Everyone needs role models. Everyone needs to be respected and acknowledged. Whether you're a leader in a small group or a large corporation, your feedback and encouragement are just like oxygen.

We'd like our health span to equal our lifespan. But staying fit takes more knowledge, concentration, focus, and practice as you get older than it did when you were younger. You need to put time aside to maintain your health.

I now have different expectations for optimizing body, mind, and soul. I need to spend more time on the soul part, through self-reflection, time with nature, and social connections with people who make me feel more myself.

If you've been living a life of purpose, driven by passion and values, then you get to a point that you no longer want to change yourself. You're satisfied with changing what you do, not who you are.

When Nancy Pelosi said, "Science is an answer to our prayers," it was a profound attempt to validate faith practice with the demands of our time. The emotionally charged position of judging opposing opinions as bad or coming from a bad place is a cognitive bias that is ruling over discourse. Having a preconception of someone can make it impossible to fairly evaluate what they are saying. The discomfort brought about by having to listen to a position that does not align with your values, beliefs, or understanding of the news can be so uncomfortable that in response we just shut it out. Intellectual dishonesty is the attack on a person's character instead of their argument.

Most human beings are encouraged to examine and adjust our positions as we grow and learn. If you change over time, it only proves you are continuing to pay attention and do the work of learning. If you did something you are ashamed of when you were fourteen, it would be very difficult to find you guilty forever or even into your twenties for that misjudgment. How we separate faith from science is a measurement of enlightenment. In America, about a third of our country distrusts science and therefore lets someone else do their research for them. Unfortunately, when you only research from one source, you risk getting propaganda, not news of proven facts.

We see the results of this from the rise and continued influence that Fox News has on our country. The most deadly result has been the disregard for CDC guidelines in handling the pandemic.

COVID-19 will forever be a signpost of before-and-after belief in scientific methods and credibility of outcomes. Certainly, this is a conversation we continue to have in this country, but it should no longer be a debate. We know that driving while drunk causes more accidents, and so we put laws in place to prohibit it and shame those who do it. We know that the virus is spread by our talking, singing, shouting, or laughing without a mask on, and so we wear a mask to protect others. It is not your right in public to be without a mask, just as it is not your right to drive while drunk. For those who say, "I pay my taxes, so I can do what I want," that has never been true, and it isn't true in the case of public health today.

We must change the conversation to make science equated with truth. Of course, we continue to learn so facts get corrected accordingly, but that doesn't make them alternative facts. It makes them formative facts.

I look forward to continuing to battle for formative facts to change what is lacking in the world. I fervently hope you will do the same.

Discussion Questions

1. Have you ever shopped at a Syms store or a similar off-price retailer? What about a factory outlet store or mall? What are your memories or impressions of shopping there? What did you like or dislike about the experience?

2. Do you remember any of the Syms TV commercials? If so, what did you think of their message? Do TV ads help you make decisions as to where to shop and what you want to buy?

3. Do you still shop at physical clothing stores or department stores, or do you prefer online shopping? What do you see as the pros and cons of each?

4. Have you ever been involved in a family business or a female-led business? Are the experiences Marcy describes in her book similar to yours?

5. Marcy describes many changes in the retail business over the last fifty years. Do you think they've been for the better or worse? How so?

6. Do you think women are still at a disadvantage when it comes to being recognized and advancing in their careers? If so, how do you think the situation could be improved?

7. If you were given a choice between a job at a large corporation and one at a family-owned business, how would you evaluate the advantages and disadvantages of each?

8. In thinking about clothing, do you think the overall range, selection, and quality have improved or worsened in your lifetime? What would your ideal shopping experience be like?

Sources

Books

Adamson, Allen P. *BrandSimple: How the Best Brands Keep It Simple and Succeed* (New York: Palgrave Macmillan), 2006.

Adler, Mortimer J. *Ten Philosophical Mistakes* (New York: Macmillan), 1985.

Arrillaga-Andreessen, Laura. *Giving 2.0: Transform Your Giving and Our World* (New York, Jossey-Bass), 2011.

Briles, Judith. *The Confidence Factor: How Self-Esteem Can Change Your Life* (New York: MasterMedia), 1990.

Cohen, Gary B. *Just Ask Leadership: Why Great Managers Always Ask the Right Questions* (New York: McGraw-Hill), 2009.

Collins, Jim. *Good to Great: Why Some Companies Make the Leap . . . And Others Don't* (New York: HarperCollins), 2001.

Dilenschneider, Robert L. *The Ultimate Guide to Power & Influence: Everything You Need to Know* (Dallas: Matt Holt Books), 2023.

Fisher, Melissa S. *Wall Street Women* (Durham, NC: Duke University Press), 2012.

Goldberg, Nieca. *Women are Not Small Men: Life-Saving Strategies for Preventing and Healing Heart Disease in Women* (New York, Ballantine), 2002.

Goldin, Claudia. *Career and Family: Women's Century-Long Journey Toward Equity* (Princeton, NJ: Princeton University Press), 2021.

Herz Brown, Fredda. *The Family Wealth Sustainability Toolkit* (New York: John Wiley), 2012.

Hone, Lucy. *Resilient Grieving: Finding Strength and Embracing Life After a Loss That Changes Everything* (The Experiment), 2017.

Kleinman, Susan. *Real Life 101: (Almost) Surviving Your First Year Out of College* (New York, MasterMedia), 1989.

Loverde, Joy. *The Complete Eldercare Planner* (New York: Three Rivers Press), 2009.

———. *Who Will Take Care of Me When I'm Old?* (New York: Da Capo), 2017.

Mansbridge, Jane J. *Why We Lost the ERA* (Chicago, University of Chicago Press), 1986.

Poza, Ernesto J., and Mary S. Daugherty. *Family Business, 4th Edition* (Nashville, Southwestern Publishing), 2014.

Roberts, Wess. *Leadership Secrets of Attila the Hun* (New York: Balance), 1990.

Sokol, Lori. *She Is Me: How Women Will Save the World* (New York: She Writes Press), 2020.

Sonnenfeld, Jeffrey A. *Concepts of Leadership* (Hanover, NH: Dartmouth Publishing Company), 1995.

Stoesz, Edgar. *Doing Good Better: How to be an Effective Board Member of a Nonprofit Organization* (New York: Good Books), 2015.

Syms, Marcy. *Mind Your Own Business and Keep It in the Family* (New York: MasterMedia), 1992.

Tierney, Thomas J., and Joel L. Fleishman. *Give Smart: Philanthropy That Gets Results* (New York: Public Affairs), 2011.

Newspaper and Magazine Articles

Behar, Richard. "Hi, This Is Sy Syms." *Forbes*, Sept. 9, 1985, pp. 30–2.

Berger, Amy H. "Business Watch '87." *Business Journal of New Jersey*, Jan. 1987.

Britton, Sharon A. "This Year Ties Lead the Way for Men and the Accent is Definitely on Fun." *Boston Sunday Globe*, March 17, 1991.

Covert, James. "Revealing Outfit: Hedge Fund Big Blasts Syms for Shady Behavior." *New York Post*, June 11, 2008.

Duhigg, Charles. "Sy Syms, Founder of Discount Chain, Dies at 83." *New York Times*, Nov. 17, 2009.

Elias, Jeremy. "Where Have All the Educated Consumers Gone?" *Tablet*, Nov. 2, 2021.

Fink, James. "Syms Store Buys Closed Alpert's Building." *Business First*, July 30, 1990.

Fitzgerald, Beth. "Syms Stays Ahead of the Retail Pack by Meeting Customer Expectations." *Newark Star-Ledger*, Apr. 9, 1997, pp. 37–8.

Furman, Phyllis. "Sy, Marcy Outrun Apparel Downturn." *Crain's New York Business*, Jan. 27, 1992, pp. 1, 41.

Gellers, Stan. "Syms Schools Consumers on Better Suits." *DNR/Daily News Record*, Apr. 23, 1997, pp. 2, 14.

Kaplan, Don. "Syms Steps Out on Park Avenue." *DNR/Daily News Record*, Nov. 22, 1996.

Kaplan, Don. "Syms Set to Embark on Major Expansion." *DNR/Daily News Record*, Apr. 25, 1997.

Lasseter, Diana G. "Sy Syms Wants to Take Syms Private." *BUSINESS News New Jersey*, Oct. 4, 1995, p. 8.

Lipowicz, Alice. "Retail's Slow Summer Tests Syms' Fiber." *Crain's New York Business*, Oct. 5, 1998, p. 40.

McQuade, Walter. "The Man Who Makes Millions on Mistakes." *Fortune*, Sept. 6, 1982, pp. 106–08, 110, 112, 116.

Miller, Stephen. "For an 'Educated Consumer,' He Discounted Designer Suits." *Wall Street Journal*, Nov. 19, 2009.

Nelson, Sharon. "Stepping Up." *Family Business*, autumn 2005.

Palmer, Jay. "Fancy Labels, Plain Prices." *Barron's*, Sept. 26, 1988, pp. 18, 20, 47.

Palmieri, Jean E. "It's Marcy's Turn to Educate the Consumers." *DNR/Daily News Record*, Apr. 29, 1998, pp. 4–5.

Peck, Liz. "The Woman Searching for the Educated Consumer." *New York Sun*, March 22, 2007.

Prial, Frank J. "Small Haberdashery Upsets U.S. Steel's Skyscraper Project." *Wall Street Journal*, Sept. 18, 1967, pp. 1, 21.

Remnick, David. "Say It Again, Sy: He's Got Educated Consumers and an Off-Price Empire, Thanks to His Late-Night Slogan." *Manhattan, inc.*, Aug. 1985.

Sabik, Cathy A. "Marcy Syms: Suited for the Retail Clothing Business." *Business Journal of New Jersey*. Oct. 1986

Syms, Marcy. "Smart Is as Smart Does." *New York Times*, Sept. 10, 2006.

Syms, Marcy. "Mom Is Still Mrs. Outside." *Family Business*, Nov. 30, 1999.

Syms, Marcy. "At the Helm: Marcy Syms." *Family Business*, March 30, 2007.

West, Melanie Grace. "Educating the Next Generation of Business Leaders." *Wall Street Journal*, Apr. 15, 2013.

Wishna, Victor. "Like Father, Like Daughter." *Avenue*, June/July 2001.

Family Business Magazine Articles by Marcy Syms

"Ask Marcy Syms: Earning Your Stripes with Dad—And the Employees." Winter 1992, vol. 3, no. 1.

"Ask Marcy Syms: A Widowed Business Owner Who Is Afraid to Retire." Spring 1992.

"Ask Marcy Syms: Ingrates or Eager Heirs? A Father's Complaint." Summer 1992.

"Ask Marcy Syms: Thou Shalt Not Become Paranoid." Winter 1993, vol. 4, no. 1.

"Ask Marcy Syms: Can Competitive Males Learn to Co-Exist?" Spring 1993, vol. 4, no. 2.

"Ask Marcy Syms: Getting Through to An Irascible Founder." Summer 1993, vol. 4, no. 3.

"Ask Marcy Syms: Advice on Asking Younger Siblings to Join the Business." Autumn 1993, vol. 4, no. 4.)

"Ask Marcy Syms: On Being Different in the Family Firm." Winter 1994, vol. 5, no. 1.

"Ask Marcy Syms: A Generational Conflict Over Selling the Business." Spring 1994, vol. 5, no. 2.

"Ask Marcy Syms: Confronting a Son Who Pads His Expenses." Summer 1994, vol. 5, no. 3.

"Ask Marcy Syms: Mourning the Loss of a Spouse and Head Chef." Autumn 1994, vol. 5, no. 4.

"Ask Marcy Syms: When Passive Owners Spring into Action." Summer 1995, vol. 6, no. 3.

"Ask Marcy Syms: What This Firm Needs Is a Great Communicator." Winter 1996, vol. 7, no. 1.

"Ask Marcy Syms: The Control Freak Manipulates Others." Spring 1996, vol. 7, no. 2.

"Ask Marcy Syms: The World Through Your Managers' Eyes." Summer 1996, vol. 7, no. 3.

"Ask Marcy Syms: A Second-Generation Leader's Mid-Life Crisis." Autumn 1996, vol. 7, no. 4.

"Ask Marcy Syms: The Best of All Possible Worlds." Winter 1997, vol. 8, no. 1.

"Ask Marcy Syms: An Offer from Dad You Can (And Should) Refuse." Spring 1997, vol. 8, no. 2.

"Ask Marcy Syms: Bridges Across the Generation Gap." Summer 1997, vol. 8, no. 3.

"Ask Marcy Syms: Mars and Venus Can Work as a Team." Autumn 1997, vol. 8, no. 4.

"Ask Marcy Syms: The Challenge of Leading Without a Baton." Spring 1998, vol. 9, no. 2.

"Ask Marcy Syms: Getting a Life After the Sale" Summer 1998, vol. 9, no. 3.

"Ask Marcy Syms: This Cousin Is an Unguided Missile." Autumn 1998, vol. 9, no. 4.

"Ask Marcy Syms: Getting Support for a Change of Heart." Spring 1999, vol. 10, no. 2.

Newspaper and Magazine Articles Without Attribution

"Syms Says Key to Running Off-Price Chain and Better-Price Sulka is to Create Image." *WWD/Women's Wear Daily*, Aug. 25, 1981.

"Marcy Syms Discusses How Retail and Her Family Business Are Entering a New Era." *BUSINESS News New Jersey*, Nov. 29, 1995, p. 25.

"Retailing Executive to Receive Award." *Asbury Park Press*, March. 30, 1997.

"The Women of Retail." *WWD/Women's Wear Daily*, May 11, 2006.

"Trump Thumper." *New York Sun*, Dec. 1, 1989

Web Sources

Syms Corp. www.references for business.com

Fortune.com, Feb. 21, 2024. "Crop Cuts"

Deloitte.com. "Women in the Boardroom: A Global Perspective."

Official Documents

Asset Purchase Agreement by and Among Filene's Basement Inc FB Leasing Services LLC and Syms LLC, July 18, 2009, Lowenstein Landler.

Annual Reports, Syms, Inc., 1983–2011.

NYSE Prospectus, 3,125,000 Shares of Syms Corp., Sept. 23, 1983.

10-K 2010 and 2011

Appendix: Syms and Filene's Stores in 2011

As of February 26, 2011, the Company had forty-seven stores and four distribution centers:

Stores (with square footage)

Fairfield, CT	43,000
Berlin, CT	38,000
Ft. Lauderdale, FL	55,000
Kendall, FL	40,000
Miami, FL	53,000
Tampa, FL	77,000
West Palm Beach, FL	112,000
Norcross, GA	69,000
Marietta, GA	77,000
Addison, IL	68,000
Rockville, MD	71,000
Norwood, MA	43,000
Southfield, MI	60,000
Paramus, NJ	77,000
Fords, NJ	36,000
Williamsville, NY	102,000
Elmsford, NY	143,000
New York, NY	64,000
New York, NY	57,000
Westbury, NY	92,000
Berwyn, PA	69,000
Houston, TX	42,000

Falls Church, VA	49,000
Aventura, FL	42,000
Chicago, IL	61,000
Chicago, IL	63,000
Boston, MA	38,000
Newton, MA	48,000
Watertown, MA	33,000
Peabody, MA	44,000
Braintree, MA	38,000
Saugus, MA	31,000
Rockville, MD	38,000
Baltimore, MD	31,000
Manhasset, NY	60,000
Flushing, NY	29,000
New York, NY	23,000
New York, NY	93,000
New York, NY	32,000
Columbus, OH	71,000
Warrensville, OH	38,000
Washington, DC	38,000
Washington, DC	45,000
Washington, DC	43,000
Atlanta, GA	49,000

Distribution centers and warehouses:

Auburn, MA	457,000
Landover, MD	22,000
Secaucus, NJ	340,000
Cherry Hill, NJ	150,000

Source: Syms 10-K for fiscal year ended Feb. 27, 2010